CVs and Freelancers

Luis R. Cerna

Bibliografische Informationen der Deutschen Nationalbibliothek:
Die Deutschen Nationalbibliothek verzeichnet diese Publikation in der
Deutschen Nationalbibliografie; detaillierte bibliografische
Daten sind im Internet über http://dnb.dnb.de abrufbar.

© 2024 Luis R. Cerna
Publisher: BoD • Books on Demand GmbH, In de Tarpen 42,
22848 Norderstedt
Print: Libri Plureos GmbH, Friedensallee 273, 22763 Hamburg

ISBN: 978-3-7597-4896-6

MIX
Papier aus verantwortungsvollen Quellen
Paper from responsible sources
FSC® C105338

Table of Contents

1. Terminology

In this publication, all professional/occupational/job title terms (like interpreter, translator, linguistic expert, etc.) are used as generic terms.

The book's title contains two terms, CV and freelancer, with polysemantic meanings in many fields.

To avoid misunderstandings, a brief overview of the terms will be given prior to the corresponding definition.

Most English postings on the web seeking linguistic freelancers ask, inter alia, for a CV as the reader can see in the following specimen for "public viewing":

Specimen	Job posting
English to German job offer, 320K words for translating, marketing (Message sent through *********.com)	

((agency)) looking for English to German translators with relevant experience in the marketing domain.
Volume: 320K words
Timeline: from mid-September until mid-October, so we will need several translators on the team
Time zone: European time zone is preferred but applicants from other time zones are welcome as well
If interested, please provide the following information in order to be considered:
- your native language and country;
- your email address;
- your updated CV with relevant marketing experience;
- years of experience in marketing;
- your capacity for translating in words per day and per week;
- your rate per source word (not per hour) for translation in EUR or USD.
A free test is mandatory.

Selected candidates must sign our NDA prior to getting the assignment.

Payment terms: 45 days end of month via bank transfer or *****.

Contact: ***@***-***.com

Thank you in advance!

The ***((agency))*** Vendor Team

The following points are not as innocent as they may look:
Capacity for translating in words per day and per week: This means the freelancer is giving stand-by time free of charge to the vendor.
Rate per source word: Most freelancers do calculate with different rates for target words. The rate always depends on the language pair and direction. The language pair EN/DE means EN>DE has one rate X and DE>EN has a different rate Y. To make it clear: For translations from EN into DE, agency A shouldn't believe that the rate is the

same as for translations from DE into EN. In this case, the calculation never works (see point 5).

A free test is mandatory: Why? This is like asking a surgeon for a free operation as a test.

Candidate must sign our NDA: This is a dictate and not good at all for freelancers.

Payment term: 45 days end of month: This is a violation of the Directive 2000/35 EC.

And some linguistic platforms offer mass mail distribution to their members for the purpose of making a deal with the freelancers (see below!). This shows a lack of knowledge and reflects perfectly the meaning of the Spanish idiom <confundir la velocidad con el tocino>, as the reader will discover at the end of the book.

Offer	Mass mail distribution on the web
Dear Translator, If you would like to send your CV to ***+ translation agencies registered at ***.com but can't afford the full price, consider investing $*** for emailing it to half of the translation agencies: https://*** If you get satisfied with the advertising campaign you may later order the mailing to the second half of the agencies using the same link. If you don't see the link right above - try turning off your ad blocker. After placing your order please e-mail us the following information by replying to this message (to *** at ***.com): 1) The text of your advertisement (a cover letter) (plain text or .html file). 2) The attachment (profile, brochure, CV etc.) (for example .pdf, up to 3 MB) - optional. 3) The subject of the e-mail message (for example, "Offering professional English to Spanish language services"). 4) The sender's name and e-mail address from which the message should be sent (for example, Best Translation Services <Best***Services@***.com> or our address: ***.com <***@***.com> or another one). 5) E-mail addresses of translation agencies which you prefer to have excluded from the mailing list (for example, your current customers). Before launching the mailing, we will first send you a sample message for you to verify if everything is fine. N.B. By registering in our directory, all translation agencies and all translators have agreed to be listed and contacted. P.S. Please note the full results of the advertising may not come immediately - some agencies may contact you in several years. Please don't hesitate to reply to this message may you have any questions	

All mass mail distribution offers on the web are essentially quite similar.

1.1 CV

CV = abbreviation for Curriculum Vitae (GB), Resume (misspelled, USA) and Résumé (correct writing, USA). The difference to German <Lebenslauf> (DIN 5008) is also briefly specified (see last column, Table 1).

Hereinafter CV is used as a generic name for Curriculum Vitae, Resume and Résumé.

Table 1	Formal components for CV in different countries			
Country		GB	USA	D
Photo		no	no	yes
Size		2-3 pages	1 page	ashap*
Age, sex, religion, family specifications, nationality		no	no	yes
Date, signature		no	no	yes
Legend: GB =Great Britain USA = United States of America D = Germany *ashap = as short as possible				

Webster's defines Curriculum Vitae as the course of one's life. A brief account of one's life. A brief statement including biographical data (for applications). And Résumé/Resume as a brief account of one's education and professional experience. Webster's New World Dictionary also as a summary of employment experience.

Oxford Advanced Dictionary: A written record of a candidate's education and the jobs the candidate has done, that a candidate sends when applying for a job.

That means, the candidate applies for a job as an employee, no matter if as part-time or full-time employee. In this case only the quality of the <employee> matters.

Considering that in the linguistic market some translators and interpreters without corresponding university degrees are active, it is easy to understand the demand of agencies for quality evidences. On the one hand, the stated requirements very often don't in any way prove that the agencies do indeed offer the necessary quality, and on the other hand must offend qualified linguistics with a university degree. Nobody asks a lawyer, architect or surgeon for a CV before engaging him for a service. Besides, agencies try to pay the same (lowest) rates to any subcontractor, and this doesn't make the situation any better. Some agencies let non-professionals do the work or service required just because they offer best rates.

1.1.1 Elements of a CV

Single elements of a CV (chronology starting always with latest element at the top) in English speaking countries:
Contact data
Personal Profile
Career objective
Work experience
Education
Skills
Interests
References.
A cover letter that stands out can be added.

The single elements of a CV in English-speaking countries in detail:

1.1.1.1 Contact data

Candidate's name on first line, address, phone, e-mail below. Special letters should be transcribed (for instance ü = ue, ñ = n) and diacritical signs (for instance accents) can be excluded.

This is critical if the last name of a linguistic experts is <Cañada> because according to the guideline it should be written <Canada>, and <Año> should be written <Ano>, <Caña> would change to <Cana>, and <Claude François> change to <Claude Francois>. The problem is, this can be construed as a falsification/forgery of the document. The penalty for falsifying documents in the UK (see sections 1-4 and section 5(1) and 5(3) Forgery and Counterfeiting Act 1981) is a maximum of 10 years imprisonment or fine or both. For other countries look on the web.

1.1.1.2 Personal profile

Also called Personal Statement or Creer Profile. Optional plus point describing the candidate and position he is seeking/applying for. It is an introductory paragraph at the beginning of the CV containing a short summary of background and career plans of the candidate. No more than 3 short sentences.

This makes sense for candidates applying for a workplace as employee.

1.1.1.3 Career objective

Optional plus point. It is a personal statement defining the specifics the candidate wishes to attain by means of professional work, the position the candidate desires. Objectives should state the candidate's goal.

This makes sense for candidates applying for a workplace as employee.

1.1.1.4 Work experience

Lists experiences in reverse chronological order, most current experience being first. Describes responsibilities in concise statements led by strong verbs. The focus is on those skills and strengths the candidate possesses and has identified as being important to his field. Branch-specific key words should be incorporated.

This makes sense for candidates applying for a workplace as employee. See below <Publication list instead of CV>.

1.1.1.5 Education

Courses of education completed. All processes or disciplines of acquiring knowledge or skill, as for a profession: Degrees, master craft(s)man's/tradesman's certificates, other certificates, school certificate.

Freelancers attach all degrees and diplomas to their contact data.

1.1.1.6 Skills

Informal education, unstructured learning or abilities through daily experiences or hobbies. Tertiary education. Language, computer, the ability to do an activity or job better, etc. helping in the profession.

This makes sense for candidates applying for a workplace as employee. See below <Publication list instead of CV>.

1.1.1.7 Interests

Candidate's contextual activities stressing teamwork ability.

This makes sense for candidates applying for a workplace as employee. A physician or lawyer has a proven teamwork ability, so does the linguistic expert.

1.1.1.8 References

A reference is someone who can answer questions about the work history, skills, abilities, and work style of the candidate. It is a statement of the qualifications of a person seeking employment. The name, position, company, contact data of the reference must be specified as in many countries it is not standard to have certificates of employment.

One thing to keep in mind with respect to the references are the possibly signed NDAs (Non-Disclosure Agreements). Some clients do not want to be named. Also, appliers must always make sure to ask clients in every single case if they would mind to be named as reference (excluding publications). If appliers do not do this, they could be violating contracts, good business practices or even legislation. See below <Publication list instead of CV>.

1.1.2 Publication list instead of CV

Agencies demanding CVs from freelancers don't appreciate the fact that freelancers, besides the confidential work they are dealing with in daily life, also may have some publications, that is to say, they may have translated some scientific, technical or similar works available to the public that document their qualification in specific specialties, that means, in certain areas of expertise or technical disciplines. In case the freelancer offers a publication list, most agencies still insist on a CV as evidence of quality. Why? Don't they have any idea about the significance of such a list?

Of course, freelancers should create their legal translation portfolio, including their latest, most impactful projects to showcase their expertise, and gather and feature letters of reference to enhance their professional standing.

Of course, freelancers should ensure their name appears in all published works (copyrights), building their reputation in the field. Branch platforms can be utilized to present an easily accessible and mangeable portfolio.

Of course, while sharing project updates on social media can be beneficial, freelancers should always observe confidentiality clauses and contractual constraints.

Of course, freelancers can include clients' testimonials in their portfolio in order to, demonstrate the quality and impact of their work to prospective clients.

Publication list (not to be confounded with "list of publication" at the end of a thesis) is the enumeration of printed (also in electronic form) bibliographical information of an author/translator and the publications involved, that means, a record of short pieces of information, such as author's and/or translator's name, title of the work, place and year of the publication and edition, often arranged in a way that makes the reading easy.

According to the prevalent convention, the list should be in reverse chronological order with the most recent publication at the top of the list.

A publication list can always be presented as it never falls under possible restrictions due to NDA agreements.

1.2 Freelancer

Spelling variations: freelancer, free-lancer, and free lancer, but also: freelance, free-lance and free lance.

The term <freelancer> means a self-employed person. The freelancer can be committed to a particular employer long-term and represented by a company or agency, which resells the freelancer's output to clients or the freelancer works independently and gets work via professional associations or the web.

Sometimes the term independent contractor may be used in some branches to specify nature, tax, and employment class of some workers. The long and the short of it is that the term is standard in culture and creative fields like music, writing acting, informatic, design, translating, illustrating, film, video, and similar productions.

Webster's Third New International Dictionary defines <Freelance(r)> as one who acts on his own responsibility without regard to party lines or deference to authority. Also, as one who pursues a profession or occupation usu. in the arts under no long-term contractual commitments to any one employer or company. Also: who is paid by the job. Webster's New World Dictionary also: who works as a writer, actor, etc. That is to say: who sells his service to individual buyers.

Cambridge Dictionary defines freelancer as someone who is not employed by any one organization but does particular pieces of work for different organizations; a person who is working on his own, not for any one employer.

Essentially, that means, a freelancer's work is an assignment the freelancer obtains from an outsourcer to be done in a pre-defined period of time.

Freelancers work at their own risk. They must have a profitability guide to follow (see point 4. Profitability).

Freelancers must indeed know the amount of money they need to get their bills paid, plus a bit extra every month. They must calculate how much they have to earn per working/productive day and how many interpreting days, words of translation, review or post-editing, etc. they need to process (elaborate) in order to obtain the calculated income. The calculated hourly rate is needed to pay for insurance, rent/mortgage, retirement plan, groceries, and more. And that's before taxes. The calculated income before taxes is not the net income (income tax and VAT must be deducted). Only after such evaluation, freelancers can decide every day if they earned enough to stay on track, or if they could even take the afternoon off to enjoy the sunny weather.

2. Qualification in Germany

The linguistic freelancer can qualify for a certain type of work by means of training, a certificate or a degree. Having two hands and ten fingers doesn't mean every human must be a good pianist. Therefore, a bilingual person won't be per se a good translator/interpreter. However, bi- or polylingual engineers, physicians, etc. can become translators/interpreters as lateral entrants.

The way to obtain the required qualification in the linguistic field depends on the specifications that a single country sets for it. That means, there are as many bureaucratic ways to obtain the qualification as there are countries in the world. The book analyses the specific case of Germany as an overview.

The background of the freelancer is as follows:

Staatlich geprüfter Übersetzer/Dolmetscher	(= state-certified translator/interpreter): Candidate can apply for a single language pair and technique (plural applications are possible) at a competent Chamber of Industry and Commerce (Industrie- und Handelskammer, for instance Darmstadt) after having completed the corresponding preparation courses.
Master Fachübersetzen Konferenzdolmetscher	(= technical translator) (= conference interpreter) FH: is one course of study for translation and one for conference interpretation at a Technical College (for instance Institut für Translation und Mehrsprachige Kommunikation, ITMK, der TH Köln, Cologne) for three languages and a technical subject.
Diplom-Übersetzer/-Dolmetscher	(= graduate translator/interpreter) Uni: is an academic course of studies (one academic course for translation, one for interpretation) at a university (for instance Heidelberg) for three languages and a technical subject.

Lateral entrants are indicated here only in a global form because there are so many possibilities as professions. As a matter of fact, they should have profound knowledge of the specific subject they have studied.

Before starting activities:
The applier must register at competent tax office of his domicile (Finanzamt) as a freelancer (Freiberufler) or as a trader (Gewerbetrebender). This is relevant for the type of taxes and fees the applier must charge and pay (for details see UStG §3a = German VAT Act, Art. 3a).
The registration at Bundesamt für Finanzen, Außenstelle Saarlouis, for a VAT registration number is imperative for traders and highly recommended for freelancers working at national and international level (for details see the web). It unveils his professionalism in tax and accounting matters.
Optional: Application as a sworn translator/interpreter at the competent Regional Court (= <Landgericht>, this is the right place to apply for in Germany) is a plus. The application demands detailed information of the applicant and the corresponding degrees must be presented at court in the original. After the ceremony, the translator

is empowered to certify his translations for official use, and the interpreter to interpret in official meetings, trials, etc.

Job posters' asking freelancers for a CV leave themselves wide open to attack in German eyes, because they act in a naïve way. And there are not enough ISO standards to iron out their missing quality and lack of knowledge. Freelancers needn't send a CV, they are already qualified by means of degrees, certificates, etc. References are only given when allowed by clients. In this case, freelancers are subject to confidentiality with clients. On the other hand, a publication list can be provided on request if the translations, the translator had done, were published. Some job outsourcers don't understand this. It may derive from the fact that CVs and references are integral part of the process of seeking employees in most English-speaking countries.

Job outsourcers' wording <you can work from home at self-paced schedule after work> can be misunderstood in Germany and in the European Union as an invitation to moonlighting. Also, it cannot be excluded that employees could be working for side jobs during office hours while working from home. And the risk of tax and social security fraud is also extreme. Tax payers won't do this.

2.1 Moonlighting definition

Moonlight originally meant to have a second job, typically secretly and at night, in addition to one's regular employment. Moonlighting is legal in every state of the US, but that doesn't mean that every employer must allow their workers to do so. In Germany, additional jobs must be declared and approved in advance.

2.2 What job posters may demand

Some demands made by job posters/outsourcers don't make much sense for freelancers. The best way to explain it is using a real example from real web life:

Example	Job post on the web
Hello, I hope you are doing well, This is *** *** senior vendor manager at *****, nice to e-meet you. We have a potential long term project kindly check the details below: Language pairs: Spanish to German (native German) Service: Translation Field: General Tool: *** Volume: The estimated work volume for the German lot is around 50.000 pages/year. It will start on 1st of January 2025 with a duration of 1 year, with the possibility of prolongation, for a max. period of five years. Also, The client wants the following:- 1. a legible copy of the degree or diploma certificate that attests a minimum of 3 years of study; 2. an updated CV; 3. Availability for testing phase that will be held online via a web-based test platform and takes place for all translators/participants simultaneously on Monday - June 17, 2024, between 10h00-11h15 (Luxembourg time). If you are interested to join us, please provide us with: 1- Updated CV 2- best rates for translation, editing and proofreading each separately for the sake of long-term collaboration. 3- Fields you can handle 4- Tools you can use 5-a legible copy of the degree or diploma certificate that attests a minimum of 3 years of study; 6- Confirm your availability for the mentioned testing phase Send us on ***@***.com	

As stated above, a CV makes sense in the case of a candidate applying for a job as an employee, but not really when you are looking for a translator with a degree/diploma. A serious translator doesn't have "best prices" like special offers or sales, he has his calculated rates (see point 4 Profitability). Dumping prices for good quality are not allowed in our economy. An agency can, of course, negotiate with the translator in order to agree on a price that satisfies both. Generally in such a case, the agency still has a profit margin (often more than 50%, see Annex 2 "Profit Margins").

What if there were no freelancer responding? The answer is simple, no freelancers, no translation. Such postings are not highlighting the vital interests of freelancers. The approach is not human-centered and not a testimony of partnership and agility. No matter how the result would be, it is up to the reader to make up his mind in this context.

3. Redefining the future role of linguistic experts

The prevailing opinion is that everyone can be a translator or an interpreter. This is completely false. The translator/interpreter needs, of course, education (studies + training) and experience as already pointed out.

A genuine love for languages and curiosity about other cultures is at the heart of being good at linguistic work. But not only.

Passion cannot be generated in isolation unless the linguistic expert is willing to learn and grow. But not only.

A good enabling environment helps where the linguistic expert has access to resources and mentors. But not only.

From the ethic point of view, the linguistic expert keeps his word always. It may seem basic, but it is not.

The linguistic expert replies to e-mails promptly. It may seem basic, but it is not.

The linguistic expert doesn't have to check his inbox every 15 minutes. It may seem basic, but it is not.

The linguistic expert works to the best of his knowledge. It may seem basic, but it is not.

The linguistic expert cannot work 24/7 (the euphemistic wording to say 24 hours, seven days a week). It seems basic, but it is not.

From the educational point of view, the linguistic expert didn't obtain his degree because he is a specialist in all fields, he is not a "know it all", but he should know the academic way of research in a new field. It may seem basic, but it is not.

If the reader recognises himself, he should think about this: Interpreters and translators have been acquiring experience and transmitting their knowledge for more than 5 millennia. The reader can understand his own strengths and weakness and motivations.

Translators/interpreters have been accompanying country and business representatives during assignments, facilitating exchanges on the expansion of civilizations and diplomatic relations, on diplomatic missions, on countless peace talks and trade negotiations, in general and in particular, in handling legal matters and interpreting in courts, on the dissemination of medicine, scientific and literary works, techniques, inventions, religion, art, music, etc.

It is not necessary to point out that translators and interpreters know what they are doing. Machines and algorithms (specially AI = algorithm incest) do not. One just can't quickly prompt a translation software to think like a German, or French, or else and expect quality output. The reader must take into consideration that translation software works mostly with internal layers in English generating a limited (English) world view. Transcreation, localisation/localization and adaption are unknown in this field (think of idioms, cultural references, systems of measurement, numerical amounts like billion or trillion, currencies, regional terms, character names and more). Translators and interpreters are important as they are able to interpolate during translation/interpreting when necessary. They have added value and that's why they are relevant and irreplaceable.

The practical linguistic experts' profession is facing significant threats from generative artificial intelligence (stressing artificial and omitting intelligence, algorithm incest, as already said), to the extent that it may metamorphose, not eliminate, its present appearance.

Prophet 1 thinks it is important to distinguish between the practical linguistic industry's overall health and the specific role of linguistic experts.

Prophet 2 considers that in the near future the traditional role of linguistic experts is likely to undergo profound changes, while the industry itself may remain robust.

Prophet 3 anticipates a shift where the conventional linguistic experts' role will largely be replaced by robots acting as machine translation post-editors, not equating to the traditional translator's role already specified.

Prophet 4 predicts a role centered around multilingual content creation and post-editing of artificial intelligence generated content.

Prophet 5 scries that a few professional linguistic experts will still work in very specialized or important areas. Therefore, their number will be too small compared to the present, and not worth to be included in any statistic.

Prophet 6 says that linguistic experts will need to completely reinvent their careers when they refuse to take on a post-editing role, fearing it may diminish their linguistic and creative skills.

Prophet 7 believes that linguistic experts will try to reinvent themselves acquiring new skills which can only be performed by humans, complementary to those required by generative artificial intelligence. In other words, linguistic experts should creatively combine these new skills with their existing expertise, like linguistic proficiency, cultural knowledge, specialization in certain fields, technical capabilities, and research abilities, conceptualizing new professional roles in line with current job market trends. With regard to this, imaginary and existing professions would appear, offering new opportunities for traditional linguistic experts.

The development in the professional world is hard to foresee and artificial intelligence (algorithm incest) cannot compete with human intelligence, but as the lyrics of the song says, nobody knows... qué será, será...

4. Profitability

Profitability must be seen in function of the country where the freelancer lives, that is to say, in function of the cost of living in the freelancer's country of residence. On the other hand, agencies registered in countries with low costs of living operating at global level cannot set the possible domestic rates for local freelancers as global standards.

4.1 Hourly rate

The common denominator to compare the linguistic experts' productivity with other professions is to convert the usual rates per day, per word into rates per hour. The calculated rate per hour is a virtual one. For translators the virtual hourly rate is approx. 67 €, and for interpreters 128 €.

4.2 Annual income and number of hours

The annual income of an employee ranges from 27,610 € to 61,356 €. A linguistic expert should not place himself below that. Thus, the minimum figure would be 51,130 € per year. A freelancer has to pay social security, health insurance, etc. from his own pocket and thus needs more money. The calculation excludes project-related extra costs and general costs.

After an initial starting phase, a freelancer should not work more than 2,000 hours per year, otherwise this will be at the expense of his family and health.

A gross working time of 2,000 hours per year includes time for project canvassing, professional training, organisation, and maintaining one's work place. A freelancer should divide this time up as follows:

Working Time per Year		
Percentage	**Task**	**Hours**
50%	Production	1,000
25%	Canvassing	500
15%	Organisation and work place maintenance	300
10%	Professional training	200

51,130 € divided by 1,000 production hours amounts to 51.13 € per production hour.

Amount of the annual performance to be sold (model of annual income depending on daily production):

Annual Performance		
in days	**in hours**	**Annual income**
67 at 768 €	402 at 128 €	51,456 €
120 at 768 €	720 at 128 €	92,160 €
167 at 768	1,002 at 128 €	128,256 €

In order to be able to earn 51,130 € per year, interpreters (basically, the numbers also apply for any linguistic expert) will have to sell 67 days at 768 €/day. If he is able to sell all available hours, the interpreter will earn a maximum of 128,256 € ceteris paribus.

Costs and VAT will have to be added to the daily rate. Calculation is different if the interpreter is not able to charge for preparation time.

Newcomers should not deviate from the calculated price, since it may prove very difficult to raise rates with a particular client, once the first project is completed. It would mean that the interpreter would have to work longer hours and do more canvassing, thus endangering his family life and health.

Interpreters are very disciplined when it comes to establishing prices: those who serve already at least 60% of direct clients will not easily be fooled by the rigmarole some agencies offer: "Please state your most competitive prices as a service provider for an agency" or "Please do not state end prices for end customers, but rather purchase prices for agencies. We will pay the agreed price without deduction". Such concessions only serve to disrupt the pricing structure. Should the interpreter agree on special conditions, he must insist on a guaranteed minimum turnover per year, e.g. a retainer.

The average of 120 sold per diem rates amounts to at least 92,160 €/year (120 days x 768 €/day = 92,160 €) keeps the interpreter busy and is highly desirable.

Hourly rates of 30.90 € to 61.50 € (or less), offered by some agencies, are not accepted by any professionally working interpreter and therefore were not taken into consideration. In order to accurately evaluate the economic damage caused by accepting such low rates, you will find the amount of the resulting minimum income below.

400 hours at 30.90 € amount to a mere 12,360 € per year. Whether clients can offer 400 hours/67 days per year, is another question. Such prices could only be considered by those, who have no background in the subject because the net value of services sold at this price reacts sensitively to the changes in the factors that determine the current income and expenditure, and because the resulting income is close to critical figures of business failure. Future market development in this sector will need to be carefully examined.

Example	Rate offered for interpreting

Job: Energy, English to German and vice versa interpretation work - please apply!

Source language(s): English and German
Target language(s): German and English

Details of the project: Hi,

We have one energy meeting for interpretation from English to German and vice versa.
Are you familiar with energy content? If yes, please apply.

Thanks,

This job is: potential.
We pay for this job: 10 EUR per hour
Who can apply: Freelancers only

Deadline for applying: *****
Contact person: *****
Company name: *****
Country: India

The job posted in the example offers 10 €/hour. In Germany, the minimum wage/legal minimum per January 1, 2024 is 12.41 €/hour. However, according to the table "Working Time per Year" at the beginning of this point 4.2, the annual income would be:

1,000 hours × 10 €/hour = 10,000 €

Under the condition that all 1,000 hours are sold to that agency (see Annex 2 "Profit Margins").

Interpreters' price dumping and agencies' greed are a bad mixture, causing much damage for the private sector. The costs for a professionally organized press conference are negligible when compared to the damage to a company's image when an international press conference is presented raggedly. More embarrassment will be the order of the day, if the interpreter (in charge) does not speak one of his working languages correctly (as seen during a state visit of a US-President to Poland).

For the sake of completeness, it should be mentioned that some interpreters may ask for daily rates (1 day = 6 interpreting hours) of 2,557 € and above, provided their field of specialization is accordingly marginalized.

For the translation sector, the following Table gives an overview of income/prices in function of the daily production in 125 days per year (see Annex 2 "Profit Margins").

Annual Income in Function of Daily Production	
5 Pages/Day in 125 Days per Year	**Annual Income**
30.90 Euro per Page (corresponding to 1.03 Euro per line)	19,312.50 Euro
46.20 Euro per Page (corresponding to 1.54 Euro per line)	28,875.00 Euro
61.50 Euro per Page (corresponding to 2.05 Euro per line)	38,437.50 Euro
81.90 Euro per Page (corresponding to 2.73 Euro per line) Hardly achievable as an average value	51.187,50 Euro
8 Pages/Day in 125 Days per Year	**Annual Income**
30.90 Euro per Page (corresponding 1.03 Euro per line)	30,900.00 Euro
46.20 Euro per Page (corresponding to 1.54 Euro per line)	46,200.00 Euro
61.50 Euro per Page (corresponding to 2.05 Euro per line) Only in niches achievable as an average value	61.500,00 Euro
Zum Preis von 81,90 Euro à Seite (entsprechend 2,73 Euro à Zeile) Hardly achievable as an average value	81.900,00 Euro
10 Pages/Day in 125 Days per Year	**Annual Income**
30.90 Euro per Page (corresponding to 1.03 Euro per line)	38.625,00 Euro
46.20 Euro per Page (corresponding to 1.54 Euro per line) Easy achievable as an average value	57.750,00 Euro
61.50 Euro per Page (corresponding to 2.05 Euro per line) Only in niches achievable as an average value	76.875,00 Euro
81.90 Euro per Page (corresponding to 2.73 Euro per line) Hardly achievable as an average value	102.375,00 Euro
16 Pages/Day in 125 Days per Year	**Annual Income**
30.90 Euro per Page (corresponding to 1.03 Euro per line) Easy achievable as an average value	61.800,00 Euro
46.20 Euro per Page (corresponding to 1.54 Euro per line) Easy achievable as an average value	92.400,00 Euro
61.50 Euro per Page (corresponding to 2.05 Euro per line) Only in niches achievable as an average value	123.000,00 Euro
81.90 Euro per Page (corresponding to 2.73 Euro per line) Hardly achievable as an average value	163.800,00 Euro

The rate per page is also given per line because at the time of first publication the rates per line were standard in Germany.

The 125 days per year are based on 1,000 productive hours (of a total of 2,000 working hours per year). That means 1,000 hours divided by 8 hours/day equals 125 productive days per year.

In conclusion, it must be emphasized that this calculation blue print based on economic aspects presents only a basic, however important component for comprehensive assessment of professional services in the freelance industry.

See "Profitability Guide for Interpreters" in: ITIA Bulletin, September 2005.
See "Fuzzy Matches und Repetitions bei Übersetzungen", Annex 1: "Rentabilitätsberechung im Übersetzerberuf". Norderstedt 2023. ISBN 978-3-7578-1259-1.

5. Localisation

Hereinafter the orthographical variant <localisation> (and accordingly the whole word family) is used.

The translator defines his minimum rate according to his experience and bibliographical search in the field of statistic material.

Not few agencies consider that the rate freelancers offer for a specific language pair translation (from language A into language B) also applies for translations from language B into language A. However, this very seldomly is the case. For further details please consult:

"The Expansion/Compression Factor in Translated Texts", in: The Annual Conference Proceedings of the Localisation Research Centre. XII. Department of Computer Science and Information Systems. University of Limerick. Ireland. ISSN 2009-0331. A reprint is added on Annex 4.

In word count terms, and as a general rule, a German text "runs" shorter than its translation into English or Spanish.

Having an expansion/compression factor it is easy to calculate a priori the approx. number of words, in other words, how much the translation will approx. cost.

Translators translating only into English or Spanish (not into both) cannot say, how much "longer" a German text will result to be when translated (into English or Spanish).

In this context, it is to emphasize that the fairy tale "translator only translate into their mother tongue" is in fact only a tale. This is a subject for a new publication.

The objective of the indicated research was to identify the corresponding expansion or compression factor in translated texts when translating from DE or EN or ES into ES or EN or DE respectively.

In the field of translation, it is very difficult to obtain a statistically significant number of examples in a certain technical field in all analyzed languages. This research was carried out on a range of 50 documents for each target language in each specialty field.

This work is very important in the translation industry for both translators/clients and those involved in the localisation industry. In translation it is important as the market is nowadays extremely price-oriented, as a result it is becoming increasingly important both for the client and the freelancer, to have at their disposal a practical guide for a reliable cost estimation.

The client needs fast quotations, and the translator has to be able to offer this on a reliable calculation basis. The indicated research can help in this regard.

In localisation it is important as most designers compose at sight in the original language (i.e. if the original manuscript is in German, the composer composes the text as it looks in German). The space is defined for German and only when the translation arrives do they realize that other languages need a different amount of space. Through applying the research the designer, lay outer, localisator, etc. would be able to calculate the space needed for each different language being localised.

The research takes into account the number of words in the source and target language(s) and their relationship.

The price of a translation varies depending on the target language, not only because there may be different rates for a particular language combination, but mainly because the number of words is not the same in the source and the target language. However, many agencies and freelancers have no idea about the expansion or compression factor involved, so how can they work out a reliable quotation for a potential client when they only have the number of words in the source language? Very simply, with following Table:

Length Correspondence			
From	Into		
	DE	EN	ES
DE	--	+20%	+35%
EN	-20%	--	+15%
ES	-35%	-15%	--

This means, a German source text of 100 words will have approx. +20% (i.e. 120 words) in English and 35% (i.e. 135 words) in Spanish and so on.

It doesn't have to be emphasized that the calculated numbers in the tables of statistic cannot be reversed intending manipulation (see Annex 4). The formula is as follows (example):

Number of words in the source language:	30,542
30,543 divided by 100 =	305.42
Number of words in the target language:	36,589
36,589 divided by 305.42 =	119.79896
119.79896 – 100 =	19.79896
19.79896 ≈	+19.80

The reader can try to "reverse" the percentages in the tables of statistic (see Annex 4). It doesn't work!

6. State of the art

On the web, especially on branch-specific forums, the freelancer sees permanently advertisings praising how to optimize their resumes and cover letters to find more and better translation agencies and so on.

There are always exciting invitations to transformative seminars and courses to unlock the next level of the freelancer translation career. The sessions are designed to provide freelancers with the insights and tools necessary to optimize their resume, cover letter, and strategies for finding more or better translation agencies. Expectations to learn are incited in all possible ways.

The responsible institutions, and forums for this kind of commercials don't say it is a wrong strategy, of course not, on the contrary, they mean they know how to craft a resume that sells. The freelancer should understand what to include and what to avoid, gain insights into what translation agencies are looking for, and pick up some essential layout tips.

They also want to reveal the secrets of a cover letter that stands out: The freelancer should learn how to compose an email that compels project managers to not only open the freelancer's resume but also to register him in the agency's database.

The institutions and forums show freelancers how to discover resources for finding translation work: They also want to share valuable resources to help freelancers find translation jobs and grow their freelancing business.

The institutions and forums emphasize that these elements are crucial for enhancing freelancer's reputation, boosting freelancer's personal brand, and securing projects with clients and agencies to get more, and better translation jobs.

The presenters have always years of experience mentoring freelance translators, and know how to lead the workshops. They have a wealth of knowledge in marketing and frequently assisted translators in refining their CVs, cover letters, online profiles, and portfolios. What else!

Testimonials are the cherry on top of the marketing cake. So, nobody should resist.

As long as a whole industry keeps making deals with best cover letters and CVs, nothing will change.

As long as both freelancers and job posters in English-speaking countries take for granted as a universal standard that freelancers must send CVs with cover letters when applying for an assignment, nothing will change.

As long as agencies are also looking for degree/diploma holder linguistic experts at the same rates they offer to non-professionals, nothing will change.

7. Invoicing

The freelancer must do his accounting and invoicing according to the national stipulations valid in the country where he is registered as a tax payer.

Each country has its essentials in this context, that's why a global overview cannot be given. Therefore, only Germany is taken into consideration in the following as an example.

When freelancing in Germany it is essential to make sure the freelancer invoices according to the valid laws in Germany in order to get paid and be prepared to handle any audits or questions from his local tax office.

Invoices are legal documents that need to include a range of important data. From the freelancer's point of view, the freelancer can receive invoices for business expenses, or issue invoices to his clients for services rendered/products delivered.

A legally correct invoice must include specific data about the freelancer, the freelancer's client, and the service or product the freelancer delivered. The following check-list specifies the data contained in impeccable invoices.

Prescribed data:	1. Freelancer's full name 2. Freelancer's business address 3. The address of the recipient of the invoice/company name 4. The name of the person receiving the invoice 5. The freelancer's VAT number 6. The issue date of the invoice 7. The consecutive invoice number 8. Description of the services rendered/products delivered 9. Quantity or scope of the services rendered/products delivered 10. Price of the services rendered/products delivered 11. Date or period in which the services were rendered/products were delivered 12. Discounts agreed on with the client, if any 13. VAT rate applied or specification on why VAT doesn't apply 14. Invoicing amount: Net amount, VAT amount, and Gross amount 15. Payment instructions and terms

Concerning point 13, the VAT can be excluded for a foreign company registered in the EU (Germany – EU) when die VAT registration Number is known. In this case, the reverse charge must be specified on the invoice (for instance: "VAT has not been charged according to Art./Section 13b, paragraph 5, UStG" or similar. That means the invoiced amount is subject to reverse charge in the country of receipt. Some equivalences for German "Steuerschuldnerschaft des Leistungsempfängers" are
EN = "Reverse Charge",
FR = "Autoliquidation",
ES = "inversión del sujeto pasivo".
Additionally, since July 1, 2010, the freelancer must send quarterly (if applicable) to his tax office a corresponding EU Client Report. For foreign companies registered in other countries (Germany – Not-EU), the exclusion of the VAT must be specified on the invoice (for instance: "Not-EU, VAT excluded" or similar).

Some agencies force the freelancer to invoice via the agency's website. The agency's format has its own prescribed data, which not necessarily is the one the authorities in Germany demand, and the freelancer uses. This is a dilemma for the freelancer, not for the agency when there is no equally matched partnership between the parties.

Writing the freelancer a second invoice for accounting purposes could be misunderstood by the tax office as two different invoices, and the freelancer can be charged for fraud and convicted. In such cases it is imperative to prior consult a lawyer or tax consulting company.

As legal prescriptions and directives can change, it is highly recommended to regularly consult the own lawyer and/or tax consulting company.

8. Payment terms

In this chapter, the legal regulations for payment due dates (and default) in Germany/EU and the ways to pay an invoice will be explained.

It is a fact, that the fee is due when the service is provided and can be demanded immediately.

8.1 Due date and default

In Germany the due date and default are ruled by Art. 286 Civil Code (consult Directive 2000/35 EC). The translation offered by Justizministerium on the web of this Article (https://www.gesetze-im-internet.de/englisch_bgb/englisch_bgb.html#p0810) is as follows (see Annex 3 "Some Legal Sources")

Section 286
Default of the obligor

(1) If the obligor fails to perform, following a dunning letter from the obligee that is made after performance is due, then the obligor will be in default as a result of the dunning letter. Bringing an action for performance and serving an order for payment in summary proceedings for a payment order are equivalent to a dunning letter.

(2) There is no need for a dunning letter if
1. a period of time defined in calendar terms has been specified,
2. performance is to be preceded by an event, and a reasonable time limit for performance has been specified in such a way that it is possible to calculate it in calendar terms from the event onwards,
3. the obligor seriously and definitively refuses performance,
4. having weighed the interests of both parties against each other, the immediate commencement of default is justified for special reasons.

(3) The obligor of a claim for payment will be in default at the latest if they do not perform within 30 days after the due date and receipt of an invoice or equivalent statement of payment; this applies to an obligor who is a consumer only if these consequences specifically have been noted in the invoice or statement of payment. If the time at which the invoice or payment statement is received by the obligor is uncertain, then an obligor who is not a consumer will be in default at the latest 30 days after the due date and receipt of the consideration.

(4) The obligor is not in default for as long as performance is not made as the result of a circumstance for which they are not responsible.

(5) Section 271a (1) to (5) applies accordingly to an agreement made in derogation from subsections (1) to (3) concerning the time at which the obligor begins to be in default.

The important point is "(2) There is no need for a dunning letter if
1. a period of time defined in calendar terms has been specified", therefore, it is imperative to specify a due date on the invoice (for instance, "to be paid before <date>" or similar). If no calendar term is specified, the client will be in default when payment is not preformed within 30 days.

The 45 days or more for payment terms that prevail in some EU countries are not covered by EU law. It is up to the freelancer how he wants to proceed in such cases.

Once again, the ineffectiveness of clauses in the terms and conditions of a translation agency that provide for a deferral of payment for more than 30 days must be stressed.

In a reverse conclusion this means that all agencies in the EU paying invoices after 30 days are automatically offenders.

In Germany, the booking day is the day the invoiced amount is paid. Booking particularities (as the legal particularities in some countries like Portugal) are not taken into consideration.

If the freelancer wants, he can wait 3 months or more for his money because the agency only pays when the end customer pays (what an unbelievable logic!).

8.2 Ways of payment

The payment can be done by means of cash, bank transfer, irrevocable SWIFT transfer, ACH transfer, BACS transfer, CHAPS transfer, cheques, bank cheques, bank draft and similar.

The best way for payments is cash on delivery (= COD). The freelancer gets his money immediately, period. This can be used for self-collectors (private clients in the same city in the fields of certified translations, interpretations, etc.) and foreign clients in a third country (freelancer from country A, client from country B, and service rendered in person in country C).

Bank transfer, also called wire transfer, and credit transfer: Is the sending of money from one bank account to another, usually (nowadays) electronically. Bank transfers can be processed via different networks. Freelancers may use this method to receive from their domestic regular clients the invoiced/charged service.

SWIFT transfer (SWIFT = Society for Worldwide Interbank Financial Telecommunication): This network is a secure messaging system used by banks worldwide to send information to one another, including bank transfer instructions. Rather than directly sending funds, the SWIFT network sends payment orders from bank A to the recipient's bank B, often through a series of other agents. Despite of what the name may suggest, SWIFT transfers may take several working days to be processed, especially if making an international bank transfer, and can involve fees from both the sending and receiving bank. To make a transfer on the SWIFT network, the sender might be asked to provide a SWIFT/BIC code.

ACH transfer (ACH = Automated Clearing House): This method refers to an electronic movement of funds from one account to another. This payment method is one of the most popular US payment systems and is commonly used for domestic bank transfers, bill payments, and direct deposits. ACH transfers will usually take several working days to be processed.

BACS transfer (BACS = Bankers Automated Clearing Services): A BACS payment is one of the most popular bank-to-bank transfer methods in the UK. BACS was formerly known for Bankers Automated Clearing Services and are operated by the major UK banks. Direct debits are the most popular use for this payment method.

CHAPS transfer (CHAPS = Clearing House Automated Payment System): This method is a high-value bank-to-bank transfer system used for larger sums in place of BACS payments in the UK. CHAPS payments are usually paid on the same day, but, therefore, will usually have higher fees.

The variant "irrevocable" for all kinds of bank transfers (when applicable) means the transfer cannot be cancelled after a defined short term. This is important for the freelancer using the services at international level for new clients.
A bank transfer can also be made via a transfer provider or via WorldRemit.

Cheques: Are documents that order a bank to pay a specific amount of money from a person's account to the person in whose name the cheque has been issued. The cheque must be covered, that means, the account of the drawer must have enough funds to cover the amount specified on the cheque, if not the payee has a problem. That's why it is not recommended in international business, it is simply too risky.

Bank cheques (cashier's checks): Are cheques from bank to bank issued to a person. They are relatively safe for the payee, because the bank rather than the purchaser is responsible for paying the amount, but still imply some risks (fraudulent banks). It is up to the freelancer to accept bank cheques in function of the country and banks involved.

Certified cheques: These are personal cheques written by the client and drawn on the client's account on which the bank certifies that the signature is genuine and that the client has sufficient funds in the account to cover the cheque (at that moment).

Bank drafts (bank cheque, teller's check and similar): These are cheques provided to a customer of a bank or acquired from a bank for remittance purposes, that is drawn by a bank, and drawn on another bank or payable through or at a bank. Bank managers in Germany advise against bank drafts due to experiences in the past.

Debit cards and credit cards can also be an option for a freelancer. It is just a question of the freelancer's business volume with the corresponding card company.

Annex 1

"CV to go"

Web platforms and mass mails

Anonymised

CV to go

Example 1

> Dear Freelance Linguist,
>
> We can offer your language services to thousands of translation agencies registered with us, if you are interested to invest in the marketing campaign, please place your order using the link below:
>
> https://***
>
> If you don't see the link right above - try turning off your ad blocker.
>
> Please note that is an investment into the future of your business and several new orders or even one of them might cover the whole your investment of $*** into the marketing campaign.
>
> After you place your order, we will get in touch with you to proceed with the performing of the campaign.
>
> Reminder: By registering in our web site, all translation agencies and all translators have agreed to be listed and contacted.
>
> Please don't hesitate to reply to this message may you have any questions.

Guess who wins?

Example 2

Dear Linguist,

If you would like to send your CV to *** translation agencies registered at *** or part of it you can book at your convenience a fraction of the full price for the corresponding percentage of the translation agencies:

If you get satisfied with the advertising campaign you may later order the mailing to another fraction of the agencies using the same link: ***((link))***

If the link doesn't work, please go to *** and click the link shown there or use "cut+paste".

After placing your order, please e-mail us the following information by replying to this message:

1) A cover letter for your advertisement (plain text or .html file).

2) The attachment (profile, brochure, CV etc.) in .pdf or equivalent, up to 3 MB.

3) The subject/head line of the e-mail message.

4) The sender's name and e-mail address from which the message should be sent.

5) E-mail addresses of translation agencies which you prefer to have excluded from the mailing list for any reason.

Before launching the mailing, we will first send you a sample message for you to verify if everything is fine.

All registered linguistic agencies and all freelancers of our list have agreed to be listed and contacted.

Right! The bank always wins.

Annex 2

"Profit Margins"

Agencies and their profits

Anonymised

Source: Author's web search and own literature

Profit margins

A. What the agency offers for interpreting

For interpreting, the example on point 4.2 offering 10 €/hour is considered from the interpreter's side:

1,000 hours × 10 €/hour =	10,000 €

Under the condition that all 1,000 hours are sold to that agency (see point 4.2), the interpreter obtains an annual income of 10,000 €.

Now the other side, i.e. the agency's side, and its profit is considered below.

B. What the agency charges for interpreting

The investigation on this case (the investigator asked for a cost estimation ceteris paribus) unveiled the rates the agency charges in such cases. The minimum rate was 100 €/hour. In other words, the agency earns min. 90 €/hour for nothing:

1,000 hours × 90 €/hour =	90,000 €

The interpreter earns 10,000 € p.a. and the agency 90,000 € p.a. through the interpreter's activity.

A commission of 10-20% would be OK, but a commission of 900% is daylight robbery.

C. Percentage calculation

The formula is as follows (example):

Amount earned by translator:	10,000
10,000 divided by 100 =	100
Amount earned by translator and agency:	10,000 + 90,000 = 100,000
100,000 divided by 100 =	1,000
1,000 − 100 =	+900
Proof:	900% of 10,000 = 90,000

D. What the agency offers for translations

Here a very illustrative example to understand the agencies' philosophy in the translation industry:

Translation Job Posting 1

Source language(s): English
Target language(s): All languages

Details of the project:
1. Accept the translation tasks assigned by the company and finish the translation jobs in strict accordance with the specific requirements.
2. Submit the files on time and ensure the translation quality.
3. We can offer $0.01 - $0.03 per source word.
This job is: already available.
Payment terms: 40 days end of month via cheque

Who can apply: Freelancers only

Deadline for applying: **/**/****

Contact person: *****
Company name: *****
Country: China
Website: *****
IP: ***.***.***.6 (N/A)
Posted on: Friday, **/**/****

Source: Web

This posting contains too many points to be objected to. Here only the income aspect is considered (see point 4.2):

For 5 pages/day in 125 days per year (1 page = approx. 220 words, 5 pages = approx. 1,100 words) the translator earns

at 0,01 $/word = 11 $	for 125 days per year =	1,375 $ p.a.
at 0,03 $/word = 33 $	for 125 days per year =	4,125 $ p.a.

For 8 pages/day in 125 days per year (1 page = approx. 220 words, 8 pages = approx. 1,760 words) the translator earns

at 0,01 $/word = 17.6 $	for 125 days per year =	2,200 $ p.a.
at 0,03 $/word = 52.8 $	for 125 days per year =	6,600 $ p.a.

For 10 pages/day in 125 days per year (1 page = approx. 220 words, 10 pages = approx. 2,200 words) the translator earns

at 0,01 $/word = 22 $	for 125 days per year =	2,750 $ p.a.
at 0,03 $/word = 66 $	for 125 days per year =	8,250 $ p.a.

For 16 pages/day in 125 days per year (1 page = approx. 220 words, 16 pages = approx. 3,520 words) the translator earns

at 0,01 $/word = 35.2 $	for 125 days per year =	4,400 $ p.a.
at 0,03 $/word = 105.6 $	for 125 days per year =	13,200 $ p.a.

Now the aspect from the other side, i.e. from the agency's side, is considered below.

E. What the agency charges for translations

The investigation on this case (the investigator asked for a cost estimation ceteris paribus) unveiled the rates the agency charges in such cases. The minimum rate was 0.20 €/source word. In other words:

For 5 pages/day (1,100 words): The agency earns for 0.01 $/source word: 0.19 $/source word (1900%)

at 0.19 $/word = 209 $	for 125 days per year =	26,125 $ p.a.

and for 0.03 $/source word: 0.17 $/source word (566.666%)

at 0.17 $/word = 187 $	for 125 days per year =	23,375 $ p.a.

The translator earns 1,375 $ p.a. or 4,125 $ p.a. and the agency 26,125 $ p.a. or 23,375 $ p.a. through the translator's activity.

For 8 pages/day (1,760 words): The agency earns for 0.01 $/source word: 0.19 $/source word (1900%)

at 0.19 $/word = 334.4 $	for 125 days per year =	41,800 $ p.a.

and for 0.03 $/source word: 0.17 $/source word

at 0.17 $/word = 299.2 $	for 125 days per year =	37,400 $ p.a.

The translator earns 2,200 $ p.a. or 6,600 $ p.a. and the agency 41,800 $ p.a. or 37,400 $ p.a. through the translator's activity.

For 10 pages/day (2,200 words): The agency earns for 0.01 $/source word: 0.19 $/source word (1900%)

at 0.19 $/word = 418 $	for 125 days per year =	52,250 $ p.a.

and for 0.03 $/source word: 0.17 $/source word (566.666%)

at 0.17 $/word = 374 $	for 125 days per year =	46,750 $ p.a.

The translator earns 2,750 $ p.a. or 8,250 $ p.a. and the agency 52,250 $ p.a. or 46,750 $ p.a. through the translator's activity.

For 16 pages/day (3,520 words): The agency earns for 0.01 $/source word: 0.19 $/source word (1900%)

at 0.19 $/word = 668.8 $	for 125 days per year =	83,600 $ p.a.

and for 0.03 $/source word: 0.17 $/source word (566.666%)

at 0.17 $/word = 598.4 $	for 125 days per year =	74,800 $ p.a.

The translator earns 4,400 $ p.a. or 13,200 $ p.a. and the agency 83,600 $ p.a. or 74,800 $ p.a. through the translator's activity.

A commission of 10-20% would be OK, but a commission of 1900% or 566.666% is daylight robbery.

F. Percentage calculation

The formula is as follows (example):

Amount earned by translator:	1,375
	4,125
1,375 divided by 100 =	13.75
4,125 divided by 100 =	41.25
Amount earned by translator and agency:	1,375 + 26,125 = 27,500
	4,125 + 23,375 = 27,500
27,500 divided by 13,75 =	2,000
27,500 divided by 41,25 =	666.6666
2,000 – 100 =	+1,900
666.6666 – 100 =	[+566.6666
Proof:	1,900% of 1,375 = 26,125
	566.6666% of 4,125 = 23,374.972 ≈ 23,375

The following example can be used for training:

Translation Job Posting 2

Hello Team 😊

Greetings from *** Team :)

We are reaching out to check, if you are available for ongoing daily projects, please check details below:

Language Pair: English <>German
Service: Translation
Rate: $0.02
Volume: 2000 to 3000 words per day
Tool: Online, we will provide access

If you are available and ready, please reply to this email with
your *** link & CV

Cheers,
*** Team

Source: Web

Annex 3

"Some Legal Sources"

Illustrative Material

German Civil Code, DE+EN

Due Date for Payment, DE

European Directive 2000/35/EC

Source: Internet, EU, German Law

Some Legal Sources

Illustrative Material

((Direkte Anfragen von potentiellen Auftraggebern))

German Civil code BGB, German

§ 286 BGB, Verzug des Schuldners

(1) Leistet der Schuldner auf eine Mahnung des Gläubigers nicht, die nach dem Eintritt der Fälligkeit erfolgt, so kommt er durch die Mahnung in Verzug. Der Mahnung stehen die Erhebung der Klage auf die Leistung sowie die Zustellung eines Mahnbescheids im Mahnverfahren gleich.

(2) Der Mahnung bedarf es nicht, wenn

1. für die Leistung eine Zeit nach dem Kalender bestimmt ist,

2. der Leistung ein Ereignis vorauszugehen hat und eine angemessene Zeit für die Leistung in der Weise bestimmt ist, dass sie sich von dem Ereignis an nach dem Kalender berechnen lässt,

3. der Schuldner die Leistung ernsthaft und endgültig verweigert,

4. aus besonderen Gründen unter Abwägung der beiderseitigen Interessen der sofortige Eintritt des Verzugs gerechtfertigt ist.

(3) Der Schuldner einer Entgeltforderung kommt spätestens in Verzug, wenn er nicht innerhalb von 30 Tagen nach Fälligkeit und Zugang einer Rechnung oder gleichwertigen Zahlungsaufstellung leistet; dies gilt gegenüber einem Schuldner, der Verbraucher ist, nur, wenn auf diese Folgen in der Rechnung oder Zahlungsaufstellung besonders hingewiesen worden ist. Wenn der Zeitpunkt des Zugangs der Rechnung oder Zahlungsaufstellung unsicher ist, kommt der Schuldner, der nicht Verbraucher ist, spätestens 30 Tage nach Fälligkeit und Empfang der Gegenleistung in Verzug.

(4) Der Schuldner kommt nicht in Verzug, solange die Leistung infolge eines Umstands unterbleibt, den er nicht zu vertreten hat.

(5) Für eine von den Absätzen 1 bis 3 abweichende Vereinbarung über den Eintritt des Verzugs gilt § 271a Absatz 1 bis 5 entsprechend.

Fußnoten

Amtlicher Hinweis:

Diese Vorschrift dient zum Teil auch der Umsetzung der Richtlinie 2000/35/EG des Europäischen Parlaments und des Rates vom 29. Juni 2000 zur Bekämpfung von Zahlungsverzug im Geschäftsverkehr (ABl. EG Nr. L 200 S. 35).

Fußnote

(+++ § 286: Zur Anwendung vgl. § 34 BGBEG +++)

Quelle: https://www.buergerliches-gesetzbuch.info/bgb/286.html
Stand: Zuletzt geändert durch Art. 1 G v. 14.3.2023 I Nr. 72
Der amtliche Hinweis nimmt Bezug auf die Richtlinie 2000/35/EG.

German Civil Code BGB, English

Section 286
Default of the obligor

---

(1) If the obligor fails to perform, following a dunning letter from the obligee that is made after performance is due, then the obligor will be in default as a result of the dunning letter. Bringing an action for performance and serving an order for payment in summary proceedings for a payment order are equivalent to a dunning letter.

(2) There is no need for a dunning letter if

1. a period of time defined in calendar terms has been specified,

2. performance is to be preceded by an event, and a reasonable time limit for performance has been specified in such a way that it is possible to calculate it in calendar terms from the event onwards,

3. the obligor seriously and definitively refuses performance,

4. having weighed the interests of both parties against each other, the immediate commencement of default is justified for special reasons.

(3) The obligor of a claim for payment will be in default at the latest if they do not perform within 30 days after the due date and receipt of an invoice or equivalent statement of payment; this applies to an obligor who is a consumer only if these consequences specifically have been noted in the invoice or statement of payment. If the time at which the invoice or payment statement is received by the obligor is uncertain, then an obligor who is not a consumer will be in default at the latest 30 days after the due date and receipt of the consideration.

(4) The obligor is not in default for as long as performance is not made as the result of a circumstance for which they are not responsible.

(5) Section 271a (1) to (5) applies accordingly to an agreement made in derogation from subsections (1) to (3) concerning the time at which the obligor begins to be in default.

The translation offered by Justizministerium on the web of § 286
(https://www.gesetze-im-internet.de/englisch_bgb/englisch_bgb.html#p0810)

Due date for payment, German

Zahlungsziel – Bundesregierung

Schon im Juli 2014 war im Portal der Bundesregierung folgendes zu lesen:
Die politische Arbeit der Bundesregierung stand während der Fußballweltmeisterschaft eher im Schatten öffentlicher Aufmerksamkeit. Umso bemerkenswerter war, dass der Bundestag am 4. Juli 2014 in zweiter und dritter Lesung ein Gesetz zur Bekämpfung von Zahlungsverzug im Geschäftsverkehr beschlossen hat. Er folgte damit einer Beschlussempfehlung des Ausschusses für Recht und Verbraucherschutz.

Mit dem Gesetz sollen private Unternehmen und staatliche Auftraggeber dazu veranlasst werden, ihre Rechnungen schneller zu bezahlen. Deshalb wurden die Verzugszinsen im Fall von überschrittenen Zahlungsfristen erhöht. Angehoben wurde der gesetzliche Verzugszins, und zwar um einen Prozentpunkt auf neun Prozentpunkte über dem Basiszinssatz. Gläubiger können bei Zahlungsverzug von säumigen Schuldnern eine Pauschalgebühr von 40 Euro erheben.

Ebenfalls geändert wurden Klauseln in den Allgemeinen Geschäftsbedingungen, die einen Zahlungsaufschub von mehr als 30 Tagen vorsehen. Diese sollen als unangemessen gelten und daher unwirksam sein. Im Falle von individuellen Vereinbarungen zu Zahlungsfristen wird ein Aufschub von mehr als 60 Tagen für die Begleichung der Rechnung in Zukunft nur wirksam sein, wenn dies für den Gläubiger nicht „grob unbillig" ist.

Once again, the ineffectiveness of clauses in the terms and conditions of a translation agency that provide for a deferral of payment for more than 30 days must be stressed.

European Directive 2000/35/EC:

The Directive on combating late payment in commercial transactions can be consulted on EUR-Lex, an official EU website (Document 32000L0035, europa.eu domain).

Latest adoption is Directive 2011/7/EU.

Annex 4

"The Expansion/Compression Factor in Translated Texts"

Source: "The Expansion/Compression Factor in Translated Texts", in: The Annual Conference Proceedings of the Localisation Research Centre. XII. Department of Computer Science and Information Systems. University of Limerick. Ireland. ISSN 2009-0331.

Expansion/Compression Factor in Translated Texts

Luis R. Cerna
***
***
Fed. Rep. of Germany
***

Abstract:

The Expansion/Compression Factor in Translated Texts
The objective of this study is to identify, scientifically, the corresponding expansion or compression factor in translated texts when translating from DE or EN or ES into EN or ES or DE respectively. In the field of translations, it is very difficult to obtain a statistically significant number of examples in a certain technical field in all analyzed languages. This research was carried out on a range of 50 documents for each target language in each specialty field. This work is very important in the translation industry for both translators/clients and those involved in the localisation industry. In translation it is important as the market is nowadays extremely price-oriented, as a result it is becoming increasingly important both for the client and the freelancer, to have at their disposal a practical guide for a reliable cost estimation. The clients need fast quotations and the translator has to be able to offer these on a reliable calculation basis. This research can help in this regard. In localisation it is important as most designers compose at sight in the original language (i.e. if the original manuscript is in German, they compose the texts as it looks in German). The space is defined for German and only when the translation arrives do they realise that other languages need a different amount of space. Through applying the research put forth in this study, the designer, layouter, localisator, etc. would be able to calculate the space needed for each different language been localised.

Keywords: Expansion, compression, space, translation, translator, freelance, client, localisation industry, designer, layouter, localisator.

The objective of the present study is to identify scientifically the corresponding expansion or compression factor in terms of the amount of words in translations from DE (German) or EN (English) or ES (Spanish, language abbreviations according to ISO 639-1) into EN or ES or DE respectively. The study is based on statistical material collected until March 2005.

The study takes into account the number of words in the source and target language and their relationship. The additional column regarding the <Characters with spaces> is reserved for further research. As to this topic, universities are welcome to continue the research. It must be pointed out that a bigger number of words doesn't necessarily mean a bigger number of characters with space nor must present the same ratio.

The translation market is nowadays extremely price-oriented so that it becomes increasingly important both for the client and the freelancer, to have at their disposal a practical guide for a reliable cost estimation. The clients need fast quotations and the translator has to be able to offer these on a reliable calculation basis.

The price of a translation varies depending on the target language, not only because there may be different rates for a particular language combination, but mainly because the number of words is not the same in the source and the target language. However, many freelancers have no idea about the expansion or compression factor involved, so how can they work out a reliable quotation for a potential client when they only have the number of words in the source language?

The Tables and specifications in the present study may offer a solution to this problem.

It has to be pointed out, that the statistical material used in the present study only refers to technical texts, that is, texts of the more general type were not taken into account.

The specialty fields of the selected texts are:
Animal nutrition, animal care, veterinary medicine, manufacturing processes and patents
Chemistry, process engineering, plant engineering and patents
Precision mechanics, automatic control systems and patents.
That means, the article does not consider <patents>, for instance, as a specialty field per se.

Basis of the statistics are 50 documented texts in each direction in each specialty field. Therefore, the total amount of documented texts in the Tables amounts to 900. The specification of the examined texts was left as quoted in the original document.

The percentage contained in the number of words in the source language in function of the number of words in the target language was determined using the following method:
Number of words in the source language divided by 100 = A
Number of words in the target language divided by A = B
B minus 100 = percentage C contained in the number of words in the source language (please observe plus or minus!)

Example 1:
Number of words in the source language: 30,542
30,542 divided by 100 = 305.42
Number of words in the target language: 36,589
36,589 divided by 305.42 = 119.79896
119.79896 – 100 = 19.79896 ~ +19.80

Example 2:
Number of words in the source language: 597
597 divided by 100 = 5.97
Number of words in the target language: 507
507 divided by 5.97 = 84.924623
84.924623 – 100 = -15.07538 ~ -15.07

The acceptable tolerance for the total amount values in the Tables is defined by ±0.2, that means that a value from -14.80% until -15.20% for translations from ES into EN can be rounded, according to the tolerance, to –15.00%

A German text «runs» shorter than its translation into English or Spanish in terms of the amount of words (see Tables!). Having an expansion/compression factor it is easy to calculate a priori the approx. number of words or how much the translation will approx. cost. Freelancers translating only into English or Spanish cannot say, how much (longer) a German text will result to be when translated. On the other hand, after reading this article, if the freelancer has to present a quotation for a German source text, he only has to consult the Tables to know, how long the translation probably will be.

Thus, the study may become a guide for the quantification of the expansion or compression factor of the translated text in function of the number of words so the translator is able to work out a reliable approx. value for the text to be translated, even when the translator has no previous experience in translating into this language. Regarding this topic, universities are welcome to add more languages and to continue the statistics.

The order of the Tables is as follows: Tables Animal Nutrition, Tables Chemistry and Tables Precision Mechanics in all selected language combinations.

RNo.	Specifications	Characters with spaces	Number of words	% Number of words
	Specialty field: Animal nutrition, animal care, veterinary medicine, manufacturing processes, patents			
0064001	Substance, O_2	1,234	231	+19.48
	Safety instructions	1,525	276	
0064002	Feed additives, Manufacturing process	6,221	762	+42.78
	Industrial standards	7,533	1,088	
0064003	Feed additives, Manufacturing process	17,828	2,185	+15.74
	Safety instructions	17,874	2,529	
0064004	Feed additives, Manufacturing process	36,121	4,426	+40.98
	Patent	44,463	6,240	
0064005	Dimetridazole, Manufacturing process	10,016	1,227	+14.42
	Safety instructions	9,820	1,404	
0064006	NPN (non-protein nitrogen) compound for ruminants	48,490	5,942	+23.01
	Patent	51,596	7,309	
0064007	Retinyl acetate, Manufacturing process	32,.940	4,036	+15.66
	Safety instructions	33,005	4,668	
0064008	Retinyl acetate, Manufacturing process	88,712	10,871	+12.92
	Storage instructions	86,945	12,276	
0064009	Feed additives, Manufacturing process	114,742	14,061	+24.34
	Patent	143,428	17,484	
0064010	Vitamin A (acetate, palmitate), Research and development	49,722	6,093	+20.58
	Report	51,854	7,347	
0064011	Vitamin D, Research and development	561,222	68,777	+19.06
	Report	518,222	81,885	
0064012	Vitamin E (acetate), Research and development	26,412	3,330	+19.70
	Report	27,544	3,986	
0064013	Vitamin B_1, Research and development	31,821	3,900	+21.33
	Report	33,187	4,732	
0064014	Vitamin B_2, Research and development	1,182,968	144,971	+23.68
	Report	1,086,852	179,300	
0064015	Vitamin B_6, Research and development	18,778	3,152	+10.34
	Report	21,348	3,478	
0064016	Vitamin B_{12}, Research and development	4,258	765	+9.15
	Report	4,800	835	
0064017	Feed additives, Manufacturing process	14,720	2,471	+10.24
	Patent	16,731	2,724	
0064018	Vitamin B_4 (choline), Research and development	57,390	9,039	+17.29
	Report	66,048	10,602	
0064019	Vitamin B_3 (pantothenic acid), Research and development	46,872	7,821	+16.53
	Report	54,377	9,114	
0064020	Biotin (co-enzyme), Research and development	66,746	8,174	+24.47
	Report	64,187	10,174	
0064021	Folic acid, Research and development	8,886	1,089	+21.21
	Report	9,350	1,320	
0064022	Nicotinic acid, Research and development	493,142	60,434	+18.72
	Report	456,123	71,749	
0064023	Vitamin C (ascorbic acid), Research and development	648,207	80,422	+18.44
	Report	605,973	95,256	
0064024	Vitamin K_3, Research and development	2,037,266	249,665	+20.17
	Report	1,870,169	300,022	
0064025	Choline chloride, Research and development	1,848,388	226,053	+18.92
	Report	1,698,207	268,812	
0064026	Calcium-d-pantothenate, Manufacturing process	363,943	44,600	+19.19
	Patent	335,498	53,160	
0064027	Thiamine hydrochloride, Manufacturing process	519,453	63,658	+21.42
	Patent	490,486	77,296	
0064028	Feed additives, Manufacturing process	947,377	116,100	+20.97
	Patent	887,228	140,450	
0064029	Thiamine hydrochloride, Distribution and marketing	40,585	4,973	+19.14
	Product information	37,919	5,925	
0064030	Riboflavin, Distribution and marketing	546,393	66,960	+20.00
	Technical leaflet	506,217	80,352	
Subtotal Percentage (A)				+599.88
Subtotal Mean Value of Percentage (A : 30 =)				+19.99

RNo.	Specifications	Characters with spaces	Number of words	% Number of words
	Expansion/compression factor for translations from German (DE) into English (EN)			
	Specialty field: Animal nutrition, animal care, veterinary medicine, manufacturing processes, patents			
0064031	Vitamin D$_3$ (cholecalciferol), Research and development	117,525	14,494	+20.08
	Report	122,563	17,405	
0064032	Vitamin E (dl-alpha-tocopheryl acetate), Research and development	14,669	2,688	+7.44
	Report	16,484	2,888	
0064033	Vitamin H (antiserrhoeic vitamin), Research and development	109,211	13,442	+18.69
	Report	104,326	15,955	
0064034	Vitamin K$_3$ (stabilised menadione sodium bisulfite)), Research and development	73,529	9,031	+18.76
	Report	76,684	10,725	
0064035	Pyridine-3-carboxylic acid, Manufacturing process	98,580	17,902	+6.96
	Patent	111,107	19,148	
0064036	N-p-(2-Amino-4-hydroxy-6-pteridinyl)-methyl amino benzoyl glutamic acid, Manufacturing process	20,497	2,808	+24.18
	Patent	21,073	3,487	
0064037	2-Hydroxyethyltrimethylammonium chloride, Manufacturing process	19,530	2,790	+23.33
	Patent	20,943	3,441	
0064038	Carotenoids for pigmentation, Research and development	70,447	10,369	+26.01
	Report	75,906	13,066	
0064039	Feed preserving agents, Research and development	48,546	6,789	+31.50
	Report	53,010	8,928	
0064040	Pyridoxine, Distribution and marketing	66,746	8,174	+24.54
	Product information	64,179	10,180	
0064041	Ammonium propionate, Research and development	83,217	11,239	+2.50
	Report	72,508	11,520	
0064042	Ammonium propionate, Distribution and marketing	38,613	6,947	+26.22
	Technical leaflet	46,500	8,769	
0064043	Sodium propionate, Research and development	56,376	10,462	+24.45
	Report	75,134	13,020	
0064044	Sodium propionate, Distribution and marketing	7,719	1,450	+25.65
	Product information	9,904	1,822	
0064045	Spoilage in compound feeds, Research and development	18,674	3,608	+23.45
	Report	24,552	4,454	
0064046	Feed phosphates, Research and development	52,284	9,439	+20.70
	Report	66,727	11,393	
0064047	Monocalcium phosphate, Manufacturing process	20,822	3,915	+23.98
	Patent	27,044	4,854	
0064048	Dicalcium phosphate, Manufacturing process	32,823	4,120	+21.21
	Patent	34,605	4,994	
0064049	Pellet binders for feedstuffs, Research and development	30,543	3,799	+21.35
	Report	32,135	4,610	
0064050	Polymethylol carbamide, Manufacturing process	15,747	2,926	+9.64
	Patent	17,817	3,208	
Subtotal Percentage (B)				+400.64
Subtotal Mean Value of Percentage (B : 20 =)				+20.03
Total Amount Percentage (C)				+1,000.52
Total Amount Mean Value of Percentage (C : 50 =)				+20.01

The mean value of percentage for translations DE => EN in the area of animal nutrition is +20.01. According to the defined tolerance it can be rounded to +20.00. Maximum divergence values here are: +2.50 and +42.78.

A text of 100 words in the source language will probably have approx. 120 words in the target language.

RNo.	Specifications	Characters with spaces	Number of words	% Number of words
	Specialty field: Animal nutrition, animal care, veterinary medicine, manufacturing processes, patents			
0064151	Device, Filter	7.130	980	+38,78
	Assembly instructions	8.180	1.360	
0064152	Device, UV lamp	29.310	3.830	+67,88
	Assembly instructions	37.260	6.430	
0064153	Device, Soil heating	19.910	3.040	+17,76
	Assembly instructions	21.080	3.580	
0064154	Water purification	20.190	2.870	+26,13
	Product information	21.650	3.620	
0064155	Cotton grades	14.840	1.970	+36,55
	Product information	16.390	2.690	
0064156	Device, Floor heating	6.720	990	+36,97
	Product information	8.310	1.356	
0064157	Feed grade urea, Research and development	14.780	2.090	+30,62
	Report	17.470	2.730	
0064158	Feed grade urea, Distribution and marketing	4.619	662	+36,10
	Product information	5.382	901	
0064159	Feed grade urea, Distribution and marketing	1.221	169	+35,50
	Application	1.438	229	
0064160	Propane-1,2-diol, Distribution and marketing	864	140	+18,57
	Application	951	166	
0064161	Filter element	620	88	+42,04
	Product information	766	125	
0064162	Filter element	5.543	772	+33,93
	Assembly instructions	6.247	1.034	
0064163	Fertilizer	6.432	898	+37,52
	Application	7.397	1.235	
0064164	Fertilizer	787	119	+37,81
	Product information	984	164	
0064165	Compound feeds	1.032	150	+42,66
	Product information	1.270	214	
0064166	Compound feeds	686	124	+7,25
	Product information	744	133	
0064167	Feed sticks	955	130	+36,15
	Metering	1.115	177	
0064168	Compound feeds	1.220	167	+30,53
	Metering	1.396	218	
0064169	Compound feeds	1.119	148	+41,21
	Metering	1.377	209	
0064170	Compound feeds	1.077	144	+43,75
	Metering	1.351	207	
0064171	Feed flakes	1.223	180	+29,44
	Metering	1.381	233	
0064172	Feed beads	1.433	211	+33,64
	Metering	1.779	282	
0064173	Forage blend	938	128	+40,59
	Application	1.131	180	
0064174	Compound feeds	2.851	394	+32,48
	Metering	3.237	522	
0064175	Compound feeds	1.205	171	+36,26
	Product information	1.555	233	
0064176	Cu Test	6.008	831	+38,14
	Instructions	6.889	1.148	
0064177	Device, UV spot	1.110	162	+40,74
	Product information	1.313	228	
0064178	Device, Day light lamp	1.423	206	+45,14
	Product information	1.724	299	
0064179	Device, pH test set	1.251	182	+24,17
	Product information	1.391	226	
0064180	Device, Special pH test set	2.421	356	+33,70
	Product information	3.006	476	
Subtotal Percentage (A)				**+1.052,01**
Subtotal Mean Value of Percentage (A : 30 =)				**+35,07**

RNo.	Specifications	Characters with spaces	Number of words	% Number of words
	Expansion/compression factor for translations from German (DE) into Spanish (ES)			Page – 2
	Specialty field: Animal nutrition, animal care, veterinary medicine, manufacturing processes, patents			
0064181	Device, Glas cleaner	310	47	+53,19
	Product information	384	71	
0064182	Magnesium test	2.785	415	+104,09
	Instructions	5.107	847	
0064183	Easy test 5 in 1	2.001	314	+14,01
	Product information	2.108	358	
0064184	Easy test 5 in 1	10.400	1.666	+18,54
	Instructions	11.316	1.975	
0064185	Mg Ca test	1.055	140	+35,71
	Warranty	1.098	190	
0064186	Device, Foamer	4.839	752	+3,98
	Instructions	5.743	782	
0064187	Nonionic emulsifying agent, Manufacturing process	191.755	25.168	+20,10
	Patent	192.691	30.227	
0064188	Device, Water pump	111.161	14.616	+19,08
	Assembly instructions	110.965	17.405	
0064189	Engine	50.040	6.542	+8,11
	Operating instructions	46.329	7.073	
0064190	Growth promoter, Manufacturing process	28.417	4.125	+35,01
	Patent	31.660	5.569	
0064191	Test set	4.125	551	+37,93
	Instructions	4.586	760	
0064192	Feedstuff	1.276	171	+43,85
	Application	1.549	246	
0064193	Vitamin blends	9.694	1.296	+52,62
	Application	12.103	1.978	
0064194	Propylene glycol	1.312	181	+38,12
	Application	1.460	250	
0064195	Filter elements	927	294	+14,96
	Product list	987	338	
0064196	Test set	13.581	1.742	+40,01
	Instructions	15.354	2.439	
0064197	Feedstuff legislation, Manufacturing process	2.997	420	+35,95
	Legal instructions	3.376	571	
0064198	Recommendations for raw material selection	2.024	225	+24,88
	Instructions	2.104	281	
0064199	Filter	1.133	155	+55,48
	Product information	1.432	241	
0064200	Results of individual material tests	5.670	770	+42,33
	Report	6.520	1.096	
Subtotal Percentage (B)				**+697,95**
Subtotal Mean Value of Percentage (B : 20 =)				**+34,89**
Total Amount Percentage (C)				**+1.749,96**
Total Amount Mean Value of Percentage (C : 50 =)				**+35,00**

The mean value of percentage for translations DE => ES in the area of animal nutrition is +35.00. According to the defined tolerance it can be rounded to +35.00. Maximum divergence values here are: +3.98 and +104.09.

A text of 100 words in the source language will probably have approx. 135 words in the target language.

RNo.	Specifications	Characters with spaces	Number of words	% Number of words
0064251	Nutrient substrates for aquarium plants	23,083	3,842	-30.35
	Application	20,306	2,676	
0064252	Gravel types for aquariums	10,305	1,618	-25.83
	Product list	9,006	1,200	
0064253	Importance of iron and trace elements for plants	8,010	1,413	-25.83
	Report	7,341	1,048	
0064254	Recommendations for raw material selection	79,853	12,912	-24.07
	Instructions	71,379	9,804	
0064255	Feedstuff legislation, Manufacturing process	31,799	5,243	-19.30
	Legal instructions	31,810	4,231	
0064256	Basic knowledges in acuaristic	39,309	6,696	-22.82
	Technical information	39,861	5,168	
0064257	Standard knowledges in acuaristic	57,939	9,779	-19.16
	Technical information	53,865	7,905	
0064258	Advanced knowledges in acuaristic	24,854	4,234	-16.22
	Technical information	24,862	3,547	
0064259	Basic knowledges in terraristic	32,147	5,476	-23.85
	Technical information	28,178	4,170	
0064260	Standard knowledges in terraristic	11,509	1,874	-19.79
	Technical information	10,014	1,503	
0064261	Recommendations for raw material selection	11,295	1,905	-26.04
	Instructions	9,925	1,409	
0064262	Feedstuff legislation, Manufacturing process	117,226	17,967	-14.85
	Legal instructions	104,308	15,298	
0064263	Growth promoter, Manufacturing process	24,087	4,103	-18.69
	Patent	24,425	3,336	
0064264	Water filter, Manufacturing process	26,186	4,462	-17.84
	Patent	26,194	3,666	
0064265	Aquarium, Power cord 250VAC EU	7,946	1,354	-16.25
	Assembly instructions	5,963	1,134	
0064266	Aquarium, Power cord 125VAC US	18,050	3,108	-18.47
	Assembly instructions	19,019	2,534	
0064267	Recommendations for raw material selection	16,045	2,734	-19.68
	Instructions	16,050	2,196	
0064268	Feedstuff legislation, Manufacturing process	33,070	5,494	-18.09
	Legal instructions	35,981	4,500	
0064269	Growth promoter, Manufacturing process	40,596	6,915	-19.36
	Patent	44,684	5,576	
0064270	Aquarium, AC modules	50,387	8,275	-13.79
	Assembly instructions	55,245	7,134	
0064271	Aquarium, AC modules	15,404	2,624	-14.94
	Assembly instructions	16,587	2,232	
0064272	Aquarium, AC modules	45,225	7,598	-4.67
	Assembly instructions	53,985	7,243	
0064273	Aquarium, AC modules	43,653	7,436	-24.96
	Assembly instructions	44,762	5,580	
0064274	Aquarium, AC modules	57,370	9,769	-27.57
	Assembly instructions	51,079	7,076	
0064275	Aquarium, AC modules	4,583	781	-19.33
	Assembly instructions	5,040	630	
0064276	Aquarium, AC modules	25,140	4,283	-15.22
	Assembly instructions	27,070	3,631	
0064277	Recommendations for raw material selection	20,753	3,535	-27.30
	Instructions	18,190	2,570	
0064278	Feedstuff legislation, Manufacturing process	34,565	5,889	-17.66
	Legal instructions	34,577	4,849	
0064279	Growth promoter, Manufacturing process	83,430	14,210	-14.14
	Patent	89,782	12,201	
0064280	Aquarium, AC modules	45,625	7,773	-22.47
	Assembly instructions	45,641	6,026	
Subtotal Percentage (A)				-598.54
Subtotal Mean Value of Percentage (A : 30 =)				-19.95

Title row: Expansion/compression factor for translations from English (EN) into German (DE) — Page – 1

Specialty field: Animal nutrition, animal care, veterinary medicine, manufacturing processes, patents

RNo.	Specifications	Characters with spaces	Number of words	% Number of words
Specialty field: Animal nutrition, animal care, veterinary medicine, manufacturing processes, patents				
0064281	Recommendations for raw material selection	35,154	5,989	-28.89
	Instructions	31,294	4,259	
0064282	Feedstuff legislation, Manufacturing process	34,565	5,889	-20.16
	Legal instructions	34,577	4,702	
0064283	Feedstuff legislation, Manufacturing process	59,055	9,811	-14.97
	Legal instructions	64,253	8,342	
0064284	Recommendations for raw material selection	32,233	5,552	-16.25
	Instructions	33,963	4,650	
0064285	Feedstuff legislation, Manufacturing process	70,614	11,085	-20.30
	Legal instructions	61,714	8,835	
0064286	CO_2 Set standard	54,888	9,681	-21.23
	Instructions	50,303	7,626	
0064287	CO_2 Set pro	83,272	13,745	-19.08
	Instructions	72,540	11,122	
0064288	Feedstuff legislation, Manufacturing process	54,720	8,848	-23.02
	Legal instructions	48,913	6,811	
0064289	Recommendations for raw material selection	73,443	12,525	-28.41
	Instructions	66,510	8,966	
0064290	Feedstuff legislation, Manufacturing process	20,515	3,273	-21.88
	Legal instructions	20,153	2,557	
0064291	Feedstuff legislation, Manufacturing process	10,202	1,577	-16.61
	Legal instructions	9,582	1,315	
0064292	Growth promoter, Manufacturing process	79,254	13,522	-11.35
	Patent	68,327	11,987	
0064293	Aquarium, AC modules	52,449	9,017	-12.01
	Assembly instructions	61,781	7,934	
0064294	Recommendations for raw material selection	32,138	5,473	-7.56
	Instructions	37,856	5,059	
0064295	Feedstuff legislation, Manufacturing process	73,014	11,085	-21.94
	Legal instructions	64,579	8,653	
0064296	Feedstuff legislation, Manufacturing process	7,191	1,296	-20.37
	Legal instructions	5,978	1.032	
0064297	Growth promoter, Manufacturing process	70,717	12,024	-28.13
	Patent	60,198	8,641	
0064298	Aquarium, AC modules	10,837	1,749	-21.50
	Assembly instructions	9,629	1,373	
0064299	Product, Manufacturing process	129,223	20,162	-20.95
	Patent	108,093	15,937	
0064300	Product, Manufacturing process	18,342	3,103	-25.39
	Patent	15,982	2,315	
Subtotal Percentage (B)				-400.00
Subtotal Mean Value of Percentage (B : 20 =)				-20.00
Total Amount Percentage (C)				-998.54
Total Amount Mean Value of Percentage (C : 50 =)				-19.97

The mean value of percentage for translations EN => DE in the area of animal nutrition is – 19.97. According to the defined tolerance it can be rounded to -20.00. Maximum divergence values here are: -4.67 and –30.35.

A text of 100 words in the source language will probably have approx. 80 words in the target language.

RNo.	Specifications	Characters with spaces	Number of words	% Number of words
0064401	Microcalcium, Distribution and marketing	10,586	1,550	+27.48
	Product information	12,152	1,976	
0064402	Cathodic protection, Manufacturing process	2,548	378	+5.55
	Instructions	2,869	399	
0064403	Recommendations for raw material selection	34,488	4,932	+5.68
	Instructions	43,020	5,212	
0064404	Feedstuff legislation, Manufacturing process	31,068	5,040	+10.81
	Legal instructions	39,852	5,585	
0064405	Liquid feedstuff additives	4,654	827	+19.59
	Report	5,853	989	
0064406	Results of corrosion tests in presence of propionic acid	3,949	597	+31.99
	Report	5,004	788	
0064407	Corn silage, Research and application	4,600	669	+33.78
	Report	5,803	895	
0064408	Basic feed, Research and application	6,444	1,022	+29.06
	Report	8,388	1,319	
0064409	Recommendations for raw material selection	4,838	727	+17.74
	Instructions	5,731	856	
0064410	Feedstuff legislation, Manufacturing process	4,219	662	+14.20
	Legal instructions	4,996	756	
0064411	Sole feed, Research and application	3,218	460	+8.04
	Report	3,477	497	
0064412	Risk of acetonaemia (ketosis)	45,878	6,804	+5.16
	Report	51,645	7,155	
0064413	Risk of corticocerebral necrosis	51,444	8,064	+7.24
	Report	59,112	8,648	
0064414	Feedstuff legislation, Manufacturing process	4,921	781	+12.16
	Legal instructions	5,536	876	
0064415	Preserved feedstuff, Field trial with broiler feed	16,886	2,433	+7.11
	Report	18,381	2,606	
0064416	Preserved feedstuff, Field trial with pig grower feed	44,676	6,768	+14.77
	Report	51,912	7,768	
0064417	Preserved feedstuff, Field trial with cattle grower feed	24,084	3,636	+8.91
	Report	30,564	3,960	
0064418	Preserved feedstuff, Field trial with pig starter feed	21,013	3,456	+13.54
	Report	25,696	3,924	
0064419	Preserved feedstuff, Field trial with feed for laying hens	29,048	4,428	+9.75
	Report	37,936	4,860	
0064420	Preserved feedstuff, Reports in the literature on fattering pigs and bulls	17,424	2,700	+8.00
	Report	21,636	2,916	
0064421	Recommendations for raw material selection	17,712	2,628	+12.33
	Instructions	21,060	2,952	
0064422	Feedstuff legislation, Manufacturing process	6,544	1,022	+8.51
	Legal instructions	8,359	1,109	
0064423	Recommendations for raw material selection	4,629	727	+8.66
	Instructions	5,932	790	
0064424	Feedstuff legislation, Manufacturing process	5,580	856	+9.34
	Legal instructions	6,422	936	
0064425	Fertility in cattle	4,838	770	+10.91
	Report	6,393	854	
0064426	Preservation of compound feeds and individual components	6,228	892	+13.00
	Report	7,495	1,008	
0064427	Free fatty acids in feedingstuffs	3,412	475	+15.58
	Report	3,744	549	
0064428	Recommendations for raw material selection	8,870	1,360	+23.16
	Instructions	10,821	1,675	
0064429	Feedstuff legislation, Manufacturing process	8,092	1,238	+11.07
	Legal instructions	9,993	1,375	
0064430	CO_2 Set pro	16,833	2,268	+45.68
	Instructions	18,936	3,304	
Subtotal Percentage (A)				**+448.80**
Subtotal Mean Value of Percentage (A : 30 =)				**+14.96**

Specialty field: Animal nutrition, animal care, veterinary medicine, manufacturing processes, patents

Expansion/compression factor for translations from English (EN) into Spanish (ES)			
Specialty field: Animal nutrition, animal care, veterinary medicine, manufacturing processes, patents			
RNo.	Specifications	Characters with spaces	Number of words	% Number of words
---	---	---	---	---
0064431	CO_2 Set standard	21,823	4,050	+17.33
	Instructions	29,084	4,752	
0064432	Recommendations for raw material selection	14,947	2,689	+19.78
	Instructions	17,784	3,221	
0064433	Feedstuff legislation, Manufacturing process	5,169	990	+25.45
	Legal instructions	6,858	1,242	
0064434	The causes of microbacterial deterioration of feedstuffs	126,612	21,258	+11.29
	Report	144,867	23,658	
0064435	Assessment of Microbacterial contamination of feedstuffs	4,651	824	+17.96
	Report	5,760	972	
0064436	Preservation of feedstuffs	17,143	3,092	+28.07
	Report	22,719	3,960	
0064437	Recommendations for raw material selection	2,653	399	+17.29
	Instructions	3,340	468	
0064438	Feedstuff legislation, Manufacturing process	3,837	604	+19.20
	Legal instructions	4,615	720	
0064439	Economics of preservation	5,904	943	+18.35
	Report	6,818	1,116	
0064440	Prevention of ketosis	5,896	964	+15.77
	Report	6,868	1,116	
006441	Prophylaxis and treatment of ketosis	21,891	3,394	+21.98
	Report	27,273	4,140	
006442	Applications for propionates in veterinary medicine	45,334	8,182	+3.03
	Report	57,859	8,430	
006443	Recommendations for raw material selection	16,189	3,207	+5.52
	Instructions	21,290	3,384	
006444	Feedstuff legislation, Manufacturing process	8,060	1,515	+9.31
	Legal instructions	10,468	1,656	
006445	Legislation affecting the use of calcium propionate in feedstuffs	16,228	3,011	+5.71
	Report	21,629	3,183	
006446	Properties of propionic acid	4,968	1,080	+20.00
	Report	5,184	1,296	
006447	Propionic acid for preserving feedstuffs	20,239	3,654	+11.33
	Report	25,830	4,068	
006448	Recommendations for raw material selection	5,976	1,123	+8.99
	Instructions	7,689	1,224	
006449	Feedstuff legislation, Manufacturing process	7,228	1,432	+10.61
	Legal instructions	9,504	1,584	
0064450	Propionic acid, applications in medicine and veterinary	13,867	2,613	+14.35
	Report	16,761	2,988	
Subtotal Percentage (B)				+301.32
Subtotal Mean Value of Percentage (B : 20 =)				+15.07
Total Amount Percentage (C)				+750.12
Total Amount Mean Value of Percentage (C : 50 =)				+15.00

The mean value of percentage for translations EN => ES in the area of animal nutrition is +15.00. According to the defined tolerance it can be rounded to +15.00. Maximum divergence values here are: +3.03 and +45.68.

A text of 100 words in the source language will probably have approx. 115 words in the target language.

RNo.	Specifications	Characters with spaces	Number of words	% Number of words
	Expansion/compression factor for translations from Spanish (ES) into German (DE)			**Page – 1**
	Specialty field: Animal nutrition, animal care, veterinary medicine, manufacturing processes, patents			
0065001	Compound feeds	15,640	2,500	-31.32
	Application	13,087	1,717	
0065002	Compound feeds	12,646	1,968	-30.49
	Application	10,761	1,368	
0065003	Recommendations for raw material selection	14,964	2,394	-27.94
	Instructions	13,026	1,725	
0065004	Feedstuff legislation, Manufacturing process	11,962	1,976	-32.34
	Legal instructions	9,819	1,337	
0065005	Introductions from the fine chemicals division, Distrib. and market.	10,320	1,755	-27.29
	Report	8,785	1,276	
0065006	Vitamins and carotenoids - core business of XXX, Distr. and m.	10,655	1,618	-28.18
	Report	9,424	1,162	
0065007	The production of fine chemicals, Distribution and marketing	10,495	1,892	-27.33
	Report	8,724	1,375	
0065008	Quality management in the XX division, Distribution and market.	9,112	1,444	-33.73
	Report	7,356	957	
0065009	Recommendations for raw material selection	23,472	3,945	-35.11
	Instructions	20,412	2,560	
0065010	Feedstuff legislation, Manufacturing process	5,515	921	-37.46
	Legal instructions	4,298	576	
0065011	CO_2 Set standard	62,298	11,188	-35.64
	Instructions	53,964	7,200	
0065012	CO_2 Set pro	3,031	482	-30.29
	Instructions	2,527	336	
0065013	Compound feeds	6,595	1,180	-32.88
	Application	5,400	792	
0065014	Research and Development in the XX division, Distr. and market.	13,716	2,448	-37.95
	Report	11,786	1,519	
0065015	Recommendations for raw material selection	22,233	3,765	-38.38
	Instructions	16,696	2,320	
0065016	Feedstuff legislation, Manufacturing process	42,609	7,617	-43.28
	Legal instructions	40,802	4,320	
0065017	Formulation methods for feed vitamin powders, Distr. and market.	52,790	9,532	-33.53
	Report	47,656	6,336	
0065018	New premix strategy, Distribution and marketing	16,437	2,995	-36.29
	Report	14,659	1,908	
0065019	Feed premixes – practical application of our strategy, D. and m.	4,845	950	-24.21
	Report	5,155	720	
0065020	Food premixes – status report and outlook, Distrib. and market.	33,019	5,472	-56.19
	Report	29,700	2,397	
0055021	Animal nutrition – technical applications, Distrib. and market.	11,152	1,231	-50.85
	Report	9,172	605	
0065022	Recommendations for raw material selection	87,141	14,241	-45.09
	Instructions	69,796	7,819	
0065023	Feedstuff legislation, Manufacturing process	10,512	1,800	-36.44
	Legal instructions	9,446	1,144	
0065024	Compound feeds	7,905	1,252	-35.62
	Application	7,596	806	
0065025	Mixing technology of solids, Distribution and marketing	55,274	9,129	-30.31
	Report	48,891	6,362	
0065026	Principals of feed premix production, Distribution and marketing	7,106	2,188	-38.48
	Report	6,674	1,346	
0065027	Recommendations for raw material selection	15,148	2,023	-40.58
	Instructions	14,572	1,202	
0065028	Feedstuff legislation, Manufacturing process	24,307	4,111	-36.27
	Legal instructions	21,578	2,620	
0065029	Compound feeds	10,310	1,735	-38.62
	Application	8,157	1,065	
0065030	Good manufacturing practices, Distribution and marketing	5,493	1.065	-18.87
	Report	5,976	864	
Subtotal Percentage (A)				**-1,050.96**
Subtotal Mean Value of Percentage (A : 30 =)				**-35.03**

RNo.	Specifications	Characters with spaces	Number of words	% Number of words
	Expansion/compression factor for translations from Spanish (ES) into German (DE)			Page – 2
	Specialty field: Animal nutrition, animal care, veterinary medicine, manufacturing processes, patents			
0065031	Quality assurance of feed vitamin premix production, Distr. and m.	10,267	1,814	-16.76
	Report	10,368	1,510	
0065032	Recommendations for raw material selection	6,271	1,137	-39.84
	Instructions	4,564	684	
0065033	Feedstuff legislation, Manufacturing process	7,704	1,274	-36.73
	Legal instructions	6,811	806	
0065034	Compound feeds	106,668	19,152	-40.04
	Application	94,644	11,484	
0065035	Choosing raw materials (delivery spec., stability), D. and m.	44,964	7,891	-26.28
	Report	38,757	5,817	
0065036	Recommendations for raw material selection	24,624	4,680	-34.61
	Instructions	19,800	3,060	
0065037	Feedstuff legislation, Manufacturing process	14,752	2,656	-33.32
	Legal instructions	12,225	1,771	
0065038	First in – first out, Distribution and marketing	45,367	7,531	-31.40
	Report	37,987	5,166	
0065039	Validation and documentation for a premix plant, D. and m.	10,051	1,569	-30.27
	Report	8,784	1,094	
0065040	Carry-over and system cleaning, Distribution and marketing	8,028	1,274	-35.63
	Report	6,876	820	
0065041	Recommendations for raw material selection	23,306	3,758	-32.20
	Instructions	20,527	2,548	
0065042	Feedstuff legislation, Manufacturing process	11,196	1,821	-37.56
	Legal instructions	8,676	1,137	
0065043	Compound feeds	10,015	1,627	-34.60
	Application	9,007	1,064	
0060544	Practical experience with bar-coding, Distribution and marketing	12,412	2,152	-36.43
	Report	10,245	1,368	
0065045	Recommendations for raw material selection	9,453	1,641	-38.87
	Instructions	7,992	1,003	
0065046	Feedstuff legislation, Manufacturing process	49,600	8,265	-38.15
	Legal instructions	43,257	5,112	
0065047	Compound feeds	2,764	518	-39.00
	Application	2,232	316	
0065048	Trends towards higher vitamins concentration mixes, Distribution and marketing	36,770	6,098	-48.18
	Report	20,052	3,160	
0065049	Recommendations for raw material selection	44,978	7,444	-34.23
	Instructions	39,909	4,896	
0065050	Feedstuff legislation, Manufacturing process	9,144	1,540	-35.06
	Legal instructions	7,430	1,000	
Subtotal Percentage (B)				-699.16
Subtotal Mean Value of Percentage (B : 20 =)				-34.96
Total Amount Percentage (C)				-1,750.12
Total Amount Mean Value of Percentage (C : 50 =)				-35.00

The mean value of percentage for translations ES => DE in the area of animal nutrition is -35.00. According to the defined tolerance it can be rounded to -35.00. Maximum divergence values here are: -16.76 and –56.19.

A text of 100 words in the source language will probably have approx. 65 words in the target language.

RNo.	Specifications	Characters with spaces	Number of words	% Number of words
0065151	Recommendations for raw material selection	11,260	1,646	-15.61
	Instructions	9,972	1,389	
0065152	Feedstuff legislation, Manufacturing process	9,328	1,545	-19.61
	Legal instructions	8,395	1,242	
0065153	Organizing a plant tour, Distribution and marketing	5,313	777	-21.36
	Instructions	4,420	611	
0065154	New standards for premix production, Distribution and marketing	9,434	1,610	-15.46
	Instructions	8,063	1,361	
0065155	Quality control methods and laboratory equipment, Distribution and marketing	10,915	1,596	-16.73
	Instructions	9,577	1,329	
0065156	Recommendations for raw material selection	5,878	989	-15.37
	Instructions	4,793	837	
0065157	Feedstuff legislation, Manufacturing process	43,042	6,292	-14.83
	Legal instructions	38,506	5,359	
0065158	CO_2 Set estandard	29,169	4,508	-19.92
	Instructions	25,735	3,610	
0065159	CO_2 Set pro	4,908	717	-14.78
	Instructions	4,425	611	
0065160	Compound feeds	7,235	1,237	-13.82
	Application	6,334	1,066	
0065161	Recommendations for raw material selection	3,206	542	-7.56
	Instructions	2,603	501	
0065162	Feedstuff legislation, Manufacturing process	7,162	1,246	-15.89
	Legal instructions	6,049	1,048	
0065163	Plant tour of animal research station, Distribution and marketing	5,961	1,062	-15.16
	Instructions	4,770	901	
0065164	Plant tour of XXX feedmill, Distribution and marketing	11,242	1,899	-14.74
	Instructions	9,402	1,619	
0065165	Production (toxicology), Manufacturing process	9,798	1,619	-14.76
	Legal instructions	8,266	1,380	
0065166	Porduction (hygiene), Manufacturing process	52,329	8,850	-15.39
	Legal instructions	44,693	7,488	
0065167	Production (pest control), Manufacturing process	1,568	253	-11.06
	Legal instructions	1,536	225	
0065168	Plant tour of the XX activities, Distribution and marketing	20,207	3,128	-16.18
	Instructions	19,099	2,622	
0065169	Recommendations for raw material selection	5,621	883	-11.43
	Instructions	4,866	782	
0065170	Feedstuff legislation, Manufacturing process	9,075	1,444	-11.77
	Legal instructions	7,102	1,274	
0065171	Production (mixer selection), Manufacturing process	23,092	3,376	-16.35
	Instructions	20,309	2,824	
0065172	Production (binder oil addition), Manufacturing process	18,478	2,898	-24.60
	Instructions	16,928	2,185	
0065173	Production (cross contamination), Manufacturing process	25,672	3,753	-15.42
	Instructions	22,852	3,174	
0065174	Production (system flush and cleaning), Manufacturing process	9,131	1,531	-25.53
	Instructions	6,913	1,140	
0065175	Production (mixer and system validation), Manufacturing process	15,322	2,240	-14.19
	Instructions	13,836	1,922	
0065176	Recommendations for raw material selection	17,112	2,493	-8.22
	Instructions	16,937	2,288	
0065177	Production (safety, personnel protections), Manufacturing process	17,742	2,594	-15.96
	Legal instructions	15,686	2,180	
0065178	Compound feeds	19,724	2,902	-10.78
	Application	19,959	2,589	
0065179	Production (dust control devices), Manufacturing process	7,769	1,136	-16.19
	Instructions	6,867	952	
0065180	Production (plant maintenance), Manufacturing process	16,458	2,410	-4.56
	Instructions	15,543	2,300	
Subtotal Percentage (A)				-453.23
Subtotal Mean Value of Percentage (A : 30 =)				-15.11

58

RNo.	Specifications	Characters with spaces	Number of words	% Number of words
Expansion/compression factor for translations from Spanish (ES) into English (EN)				
Specialty field: Animal nutrition, animal care, veterinary medicine, manufacturing processes, patents				
0065181	Production (labels, identification), Manufacturing process	6,348	1,039	-15.88
	Legal instructions	5,832	874	
0065182	Medicohygienic effects of propionic acid in animal feeds	7,488	1,186	-14.67
	Report	6,890	1,012	
0065183	Propylene glycol in animal nutrition	12,696	2,116	-14.36
	Report	11,187	1,812	
0065184	Propylene glycol as preservative	20,368	3,496	-14.30
	Report	17,503	2,996	
0065185	Production (retain samples), Manufacturing process	4,885	809	-14.71
	Legal instructions	4,498	690	
0065186	Production (packaging requirements), Manufacturing process	95,229	15,782	-24.19
	Legal instructions	84,966	11,964	
0065187	Propylene glycol as energy carrier	6,619	1,062	-16.48
	Report	5,313	887	
0065188	Recommendations for raw material selection	7,387	1,136	-16.20
	Instructions	6,550	952	
0065189	Feedstuff legislation, Manufacturing process	1,108	161	-16.15
	Legal instructions	979	135	
0065190	Propylene glycol as dust binder	6,900	1,090	-9.26
	Report	5,957	989	
0065191	Propylene glycol as humectant	5,759	966	-15.32
	Report	4,733	818	
0065192	Recommendations for raw material selection	2,783	464	-13.79
	Instructions	2,378	400	
0065193	Feedstuff legislation, Manufacturing process	3,956	694	-15.27
	Legal instructions	3,321	588	
0065194	Propylene glycol as antifoaming agent	4,232	717	-12.83
	Report	3,799	625	
0065195	Incorporation of propylene glycol in mixed feeds	5,630	938	-15.67
	Report	4,977	791	
0065196	Analitical determination of propylene glycol	5,336	869	-12.66
	Report	4,871	759	
0065197	Device, Water pump	76,452	13,321	-14.22
	Assembly instructions	63,912	11,426	
0065198	Recommendations for raw material selection	4,784	809	-13.60
	Instructions	4,218	699	
0065199	Feedstuff legislation, Manufacturing process	37,752	6,403	-14.59
	Legal instructions	32,540	5,469	
0065200	Iron test set	5,589	989	-13.95
	Instructions	4,945	851	
Subtotal Percentage (B)				-298.10
Subtotal Mean Value of Percentage (B : 20 =)				-14.90
Total Amount Percentage (C)				-751.33
Total Amount Mean Value of Percentage (C : 50 =)				-15.03

The mean value of percentage for translations ES => EN in the area of animal nutrition is – 15.03. According to the defined tolerance it can be rounded to -15.00. Maximum divergence values here are: -4.56 and –25.53.

A text of 100 words in the source language will probably have approx. 85 words in the target language.

RNo.	Specifications	Characters with spaces	Number of words	% Number of words
	Expansion/compression factor for translations from German (DE) into English (EN)			Page – 1
	Specialty field: Chemistry, process engineering, plant engineering, patents			
9582001	Production plant	7,177	879	+24.57
	Safety instructions	6,901	1,095	
9582002	Substance, Manufacturing process	58,752	7,200	+20.00
	Patent	54,432	8,640	
9582003	Device, Servo motor	43,640	5,348	+21.06
	Assembly instructions	40,774	6,472	
9582004	Plant engineering, Production plant	1,018,686	124,839	+21.30
	Assembly instructions	954,009	151,430	
9582005	Device, Compact AC servo motor	558,552	68,450	+22.30
	Patent	527,405	83,715	
9582006	Production plant	391,337	47,958	+19.40
	Assembly instructions	360,751	57,262	
9582007	Device, Filter regulator	1,987,515	243,568	+19.00
	Set up instructions	1,826,030	289,846	
9582008	Substance, Manufacturing process	2,190,609	268,457	+18.90
	Patent	2,010,935	319,196	
9582009	Substance, Manufacturing process	696,997	86,476	+19.60
	Patent	651,584	103,426	
9582010	Device, Solenoid valves	530,261	64,983	+19.80
	Safety instructions	490,455	77,850	
9582011	Production plant	603,465	73,954	+19.60
	Assembly instructions	557,229	88,449	
9582012	Substance, Manufacturing process	53,465	6,552	+20,88
	Patent	55,758	7,920	
9582013	Production plant	123,379	15,120	+25.00
	Assembly instructions, Machine instalation	154,224	18,900	
9582014	Substance, Manufacturing process	9,539	1,169	+13.60
	Safety instructions	9,349	1,328	
9582015	Production plant	3,542	434	+16.13
	Assembly instructions	3,549	504	
9582016	Substance, Manufacturing process	5,214	639	+23.32
	Industrial standards	5,548	788	
9582017	Substance, Manufacturing process	1,077	132	+13.64
	Industrial standards	1,056	150	
9582018	Substance, Manufacturing process	3,884	476	+42.65
	Industrial standards	4,781	679	
9582019	Device, Air lines for pneumatic installation	1,917	235	+16.17
	Safety instructions	1,922	273	
9582020	Device, Pneumatic presser	669	82	+40.24
	Assembly instructions	810	115	
9582021	Substance, Manufacturing process	9,555	1,171	+21.95
	Industrial standards	10,054	1,428	
9582022	Substance, Manufacturing process	71,770	8,790	+24.57
	Patent	69,019	10,950	
9582023	Substance, Manufacturing process	5,040	841	+16.88
	Industrial standards	5,847	983	
9582024	Device, Driving system	6,171	972	+17.90
	Assembly instructions	7,102	1,146	
9852025	Substance, Manufacturing process	15,828	2,657	+10.58
	Patent	17,991	2,938	
9582026	Substance, Manufacturing process	4,579	823	+8.63
	Instructions	5,162	894	
9582027	Substance, Manufacturing process	20,192	3,390	+10.59
	Patent	22,955	3,749	
9582028	Substance, Manufacturing process	1,272,009	155,883	+19.00
	Patent	1,168,659	185,502	
9582029	Substance, Manufacturing process	34,217	4,194	+23.24
	Instructions	35,685	5,069	
9582030	Device, Electric wiper	28,400	3,581	+11.90
	Assembly instructions	29,618	4,007	
Subtotal Percentage (A)				+602.40
Subtotal Mean Value of Percentage (A : 30 =)				+20.08

	Expansion/compression factor for translations from German (DE) into English (EN)			Page – 2
	Specialty field: Chemistry, process engineering, plant engineering, patents			
RNo.	Specifications	Characters with spaces	Number of words	% Number of words
9582031	Substance, Manufacturing process	89,481	12,186	+0.83
	Patent	77,966	12,287	
9582032	Device, Indications of danger, warnings and cautions	5,220	730	+30.14
	Industrial standards	5,700	950	
9582033	Device, Symbols and messages	7,575	1,115	+25.47
	Industrial standards	8,162	1,399	
9582034	Device, Safety precautions	2,100	300	+20.00
	Industrial standards	2,252	360	
9582035	Device, Maintenance, check, repair	2,204	302	+20.86
	Instructions	2,266	365	
9582036	Device, Maintenance	10,600	1,925	+8.52
	Instructions	11,947	2,089	
9582037	Device, Manual switch	79,064	9,711	+20.82
	Assembly instructions	82,456	11,733	
9582038	Device, Connecting power relay cord	117,432	14,454	+20.77
	Instructions	112,179	17,456	
9582039	Device, Replacing and ajusting knives	15,774	2,891	+8.47
	Instructions	17,725	3,136	
9582040	Device, Blade overlap adjustment	126,371	15,586	+20.72
	Instructions	131,789	18,816	
9582041	Device, Adjusting pressure	22,095	2,729	+21.73
	Instructions	23,248	3,322	
9582042	Substance, Manufacturing process	16,933	3,147	+8.36
	Instructions	19,159	3,410	
9582043	Device, Adjusting the differential feed ratio	32,842	4,085	+21.59
	Instructions	34,554	4,967	
9582044	Device, Changing the specifications	35,294	4,431	+21.42
	Instructions	37,210	5,380	
9582045	Substance, Manufacturing process	2,239	421	+23.75
	Instructions	2,908	521	
9582046	Device, Replacing fuse of controller	5,622	1,015	+26.70
	Instructions	7,175	1,286	
9582047	Device, Safety labels	2,008	388	+20.87
	Industrial standards	2,640	469	
9582048	Substance, Manufacturing process	830	156	+26.28
	Instructions	1,068	197	
9582049	Device, Installing the belt cover	6.062	1,125	+23.56
	Instructions	8,079	1,390	
9582050	Device, Lubrication	4,152	747	+26.37
	Instructions	5,000	944	
Subtotal Percentage (B)				**+397.23**
Subtotal Mean Value of Percentage (B : 20 =)				**+19.86**
Total Amount Percentage (C)				**+999.63**
Total Amount Mean Value of Percentage (C : 50 =)				**+19.99**

The mean value of percentage for translations DE => EN in the area of chemistry is +19.99. According to the defined tolerance it can be rounded to +20.00. Maximum divergence values here are: +42.65 and +0.83.

A text of 100 words in the source language will probably have approx. 120 words in the target language.

RNo.	Specifications	Characters with spaces	Number of words	% Number of words
	Expansion/compression factor for translations from German (DE) into Spanish (ES)			Page – 1
	Specialty field: Chemistry, process engineering, plant engineering, patents			
9582151	Substance, Manufacturing process	34,621	4,672	+22.83
	Patent	35,503	5,739	
9582152	Substance, Manufacturing process	99,473	12,716	+30.72
	Patent	105,019	16,623	
9582153	Substance, Manufacturing process	60,085	7,841	+21.45
	Patent	61,901	9,523	
9582154	Substance, Manufacturing process	48,301	6,235	+24.47
	Patent	49,414	7,761	
9582155	Substance, Manufacturing process	207,850	29,780	+40.73
	Patent	236,050	41,910	
9582156	Safety regulations	10,410	1,528	+38.61
	Prevention of accidents	11,891	2,118	
9582157	Substance, Manufacturing process	285,487	36,494	+30.73
	Production	301,404	47,709	
9582158	Substance, Manufacturing process	35,706	5,240	+38.64
	Production	40,787	7,265	
9582159	Substance, Manufacturing process	74,826	10,720	+40.75
	Production	84,978	15,089	
9582160	Substance, Manufacturing process	80,593	11,547	+40.70
	Patent	91,519	16,247	
9582161	Substance, Manufacturing process	22,852	2,888	+22.02
	Patent	23,760	3,524	
9582162	Substance, Manufacturing process	24,731	3,114	+21.83
	Production	25,529	3,794	
9582163	Substance, Manufacturing process	42,369	4,601	+19.12
	Production	43,456	5,481	
9582164	Substance, Manufacturing process	47,070	4,970	+17.26
	Production	47,988	5,828	
9582165	Substance, Manufacturing process	55,477	5,916	+16.36
	Patent	56,829	6,884	
9582166	Substance, Manufacturing process	14,980	2,363	+31.52
	Production	17,305	3,108	
9582167	Substance, Manufacturing process	10,290	1,510	+39.07
	Production	12,520	2,100	
9592168	Substance, Manufacturing process	7,220	1,020	+48.04
	Patent	8,600	1,510	
9582169	Substance, Manufacturing process	5,170	790	+27.85
	Production	6,050	1,010	
9582170	Substance, Manufacturing process	826	109	+43.12
	Production	920	156	
9582171	Substance, Manufacturing process	1,059	151	+25.16
	Production	1,160	189	
9582172	Substance, Manufacturing process	10,820	1,400	+45.71
	Patent	12,240	2,040	
9582173	Substance, Manufacturing process	8,970	1,220	+53.28
	Patent	10,730	1,870	
9582174	Substance, Manufacturing process	9,170	1,190	+47.90
	Production	10,400	1,760	
9582175	Substance, Manufacturing process	7,074	953	+46.06
	Production	8,207	1,392	
9582176	Substance, Manufacturing process	10,750	1,640	+31.10
	Patent	12,150	2,150	
9582177	Substance, Manufacturing process	1,498	201	+28.36
	Production	1,628	258	
9582178	Substance, Manufacturing process	126,800	17,200	+31.39
	Patent	138,000	22,600	
9582179	Substance, Manufacturing process	2,432	355	+29.58
	Production	2,760	460	
9582180	Substance, Manufacturing process	38,050	4,990	+52.30
	Patent	44,280	7,600	
Subtotal Percentage (A)				**+1,006.66**
Subtotal Mean Value of Percentage (A : 30 =)				**+33.55**

RNo.	Specifications	Characters with spaces	Number of words	% Number of words
Specialty field: Chemistry, process engineering, plant engineering, patents				
9582181	Substance, Manufacturing process	97,800	14,100	+24.82
	Patent	106,200	17,600	
9582182	Substance, Manufacturing process	18,471	2,421	+41.72
	Production	20,702	3,431	
9582183	Substance, Manufacturing process	1,155	159	+45.28
	Production	1,439	231	
9582184	Substance, Manufacturing process	213	29	+20.69
	Production	241	35	
9582185	Substance, Manufacturing process	14,240	1,890	+30.69
	Patent	16,060	2,470	
9582186	Substance, Manufacturing process	566	77	+53.25
	Production	697	118	
9582187	Plant engineering	1,295	176	+34.66
	Production	1,500	237	
9582188	Substance, Manufacturing process	10,370	1,470	+57.14
	Patent	12,960	2,310	
9582189	Substance, Manufacturing process	1,315	189	+43.39
	Production	1,557	271	
9582190	Substance, Manufacturing process	9,716	1,348	+42.73
	Patent	11,376	1,924	
9582191	Substance, Manufacturing process	1,797	261	+34.86
	Production	2,130	352	
9582192	Plant engineering	2,044	303	+36.30
	Production	2,444	413	
9582193	Substance, Manufacturing process	3,340	500	+34.00
	Production	3,910	670	
9582194	Plant engineering	4,152	532	+27.82
	Production	4,393	680	
9582195	Plant engineering	1,058	151	+27.15
	Production	1,222	192	
9582196	Substance, Manufacturing process	1,544	208	+50.96
	Production	1,973	314	
9582197	Substance, Manufacturing process	18,250	2,600	+29.23
	Patent	20,280	3,360	
9582198	Plant engineering	1,753	267	+31.09
	Production	2,051	350	
9582199	Substance, Manufacturing process	10,420	1,530	+40.52
	Patent	12,780	2,150	
9582200	Plant engineering	13,770	1,960	+37.24
	Production	15,730	2,690	
Subtotal Percentage (B)				+743.54
Subtotal Mean Value of Percentage (B : 20 =)				+37.18
Total Amount Percentage (C)				+1,750.20
Total Amount Mean Value of Percentage (C : 50 =)				+35.00

The mean value of percentage for translations DE => ES in the area of chemistry is +35.00. According to the defined tolerance it can be rounded to +35.00. Maximum divergence values here are: +57.14 and +16.36.

A text of 100 words in the source language will probably have approx. 135 words in the target language.

RNo.	Specifications	Characters with spaces	Number of words	% Number of words
	Specialty field: Chemistry, process engineering, plant engineering, patents			
9582251	Substance, Manufacturing process	100,710	17,315	-11.41
	Patent	118,630	15,340	
9582252	Substance, Manufacturing process	6,171	1,051	-5.80
	Safety instructions	7,269	990	
9582253	Production plant	1,526	260	-40.00
	Safety instructions	1,145	156	
9582254	Substance, Manufacturing process	34,660	5,970	-15.07
	Patent	36,520	5,070	
9582255	Device, Power stearing	3,081	525	-20.00
	Safety instructions	3,082	420	
9582256	Substance, Manufacturing process	63,500	10,550	-14.69
	Patent	69,090	9,000	
9582257	Plant engineering	7,795	1,328	-11.97
	Safety instructions	8,580	1,169	
9582258	Substance, Manufacturing process	9,675	1,589	-14.22
	Industrial standards	10,608	1,363	
9582259	Substance, Manufacturing process	2,958	504	-13.89
	Safety instructions	3,185	434	
9582260	Device, Belt cover	8,684	1,459	-3.36
	Assembly instructions	10,366	1,410	
9582261	Substance, Manufacturing process	4,625	788	-18.91
	Safety instructions	4,690	639	
9582262	Device, Handwheel	50,281	8,568	-23.39
	Assembly instructions	50,298	6,564	
9582263	Substance, Manufacturing process	880	150	-12.00
	Safety instructions	968	132	
9582264	Substance, Manufacturing process	48,274	8,225	-14.33
	Patent	51,979	7,046	
9582265	Plant engineering	3,985	679	-29.90
	Safety instructions	3,493	476	
9582266	Substance, Manufacturing process	66,370	11,309	-20.82
	Patent	66,393	8,954	
9582267	Plant engineering	1,602	273	-13.92
	Safety instructions	1,724	235	
9582268	Substance, Manufacturing process	87,608	14,927	-22.59
	Patent	87,638	11,555	
9582269	Plant engineering	675	115	-28.70
	Safety instructions	601	82	
9582270	Substance, Manufacturing process	66,370	11,309	-20.65
	Patent	66,394	8,974	
9582271	Substance, Manufacturing process	8,382	1,428	-25.00
	Safety instructions	8,595	1,071	
9582272	Plant engineering	11,016	1,876	-28.68
	Safety instructions	9,808	1,338	
9582273	Substance, Manufacturing process	61,060	10,404	-21.61
	Patent	61,082	8,156	
9582274	Plant engineering	75,480	12,860	-21.45
	Assembly instructions	76,540	10,102	
9582275	Substance, Manufacturing process	11,125	1,878	-20.07
	Safety instructions	10,343	1,501	
9582276	Substance, Manufacturing process	47,724	8,132	-22.71
	Patent	47,740	6,285	
9582277	Plant engineering	61,727	10,517	-28.94
	Assembly instructions	54,106	7,473	
9582278	Substance, Manufacturing process	2,210	360	-24.72
	Safety instructions	1,923	271	
9582279	Substance, Manufacturing process	2,169	366	-30.87
	Safety instructions	1,906	253	
9582280	Device, Auxiliary motor	2,251	345	-20.00
	Specifications label	2,003	276	
Subtotal Percentage (A)				-599.67
Subtotal Mean Value of Percentage (A : 30 =)				-19.99

	Specialty field: Chemistry, process engineering, plant engineering, patents			
RNo.	Specifications	Characters with spaces	Number of words	% Number of words
9582281	Substance, Manufacturing process	1,271	217	-19.82
	Safety instructions	1,200	174	
9582282	Substance, Manufacturing process	1,602	250	-21.60
	Safety instructions	1,340	196	
9582283	Substance, Manufacturing process	35,220	5,960	-25.67
	Patent	30,690	4,430	
9582284	Substance, Manufacturing process	24,814	3,872	-21.33
	Patent	20,756	3,046	
9582285	Substance, Manufacturing process	2,081	336	-19.05
	Safety instructions	1,849	272	
9582286	Device, Auxiliary motor	1,358	231	-26.41
	Specifications label	1,156	170	
9582287	Plant engineering	1,381	249	-19.28
	Safety instructions	1,148	201	
9582288	Substance, Manufacturing process	1,402	213	-18,78
	Safety instructions	1,240	173	
9582289	Plant engineering	1,199	190	-23.16
	Safety instructions	968	146	
9582290	Substance, Manufacturing process	1,574	260	-20.77
	Safety instructions	1,292	206	
9582291	Substance, Manufacturing process	1,664	259	-22.78
	Safety instructions	1,416	200	
9582292	Plant engineering	2,058	329	-19.15
	Safety instructions	1,722	266	
9582293	Plant engineering	1,356	213	-16.43
	Safety instructions	1,185	178	
9582294	Substance, Manufacturing process	1,054	186	-20.43
	Safety instructions	966	148	
9582295	Plant engineering	1,599	264	-19.70
	Safety instructions	1,393	212	
9582296	Substance, Manufacturing process	10,507	1,699	-18.19
	Transport instructions	9,392	1,390	
9582297	Substance, Manufacturing process	14,102	2,405	-19.17
	Patent	12,771	1,944	
9582298	Substance, Manufacturing process	394	63	-19.05
	Safety instructions	387	51	
9582299	Plant engineering	1,959	303	-16.50
	Safety instructions	1,840	253	
9582300	Substance, Manufacturing process	15,218	2,597	-12.71
	Patent	13,120	2,267	
Subtotal Percentage (B)				-399.98
Subtotal Mean Value of Percentage (B : 20 =)				-19.99
Total Amount Percentage (C)				-999.65
Total Amount Mean Value of Percentage (C : 50 =)				-19.99

The mean value of percentage for translations EN => DE in the area of chemistry is –19.99. According to the defined tolerance it can be rounded to -20.00. Maximum divergence values here are: -3.36 and –40.00.

A text of 100 words in the source language will probably have approx. 80 words in the target language.

RNo.	Specifications	Characters with spaces	Number of words	% Number of words
	Expansion/compression factor for translations from English (EN) into Spanish (ES)			**Page – 1**
	Specialty field: Chemistry, process engineering, plant engineering, patents			
9582401	Substance, Manufacturing process	35,267	5,905	+10.82
	Patent	40,241	6,544	
9582402	Substance, Manufacturing process	4,676	630	+45.40
	Production	5,260	916	
9582403	Substance, Manufacturing process	1,124	172	+5.23
	Safety instructions	1,388	181	
9582404	Production plant	1,232	189	+13.23
	Safety instructions	1,503	214	
9582405	Safety instructions	474	66	+15.15
	Safety instructions	520	76	
9582406	Production plant	865	124	+16.13
	Safety instructions	1,041	144	
9582407	Production plant	672	107	+26.16
	Safety instructions	888	135	
9582408	Production plant	775	119	+11.76
	Safety instructions	892	133	
9582409	Production plant	643	101	+29.70
	Safety instructions	824	130	
9582410	Production plant	909	142	+22.53
	Safety instructions	1,161	174	
9582411	Production plant	447	64	+6.25
	Safety instructions	483	68	
9582412	Production plant	586	92	+15.21
	Safety instructions	694	106	
9582413	Production plant	672	101	+16.83
	Safety instructions	796	118	
9582414	Production plant	895	142	+28.87
	Safety instructions	1,165	183	
9582415	Production plant	639	93	+33.33
	Safety instructions	806	124	
9582416	Production plant	1,097	166	+31.32
	Safety instructions	1,390	218	
9582417	Production plant	1,293	202	+22.27
	Safety instructions	1,626	247	
9582418	Substance, Manufacturing process	8630	1,400	+12.86
	Industrial standards	11,070	1,580	
9582419	Device, Pneumatic pump	9,580	1,370	+3.65
	Assembly instructions	11,950	1,420	
9582420	Production plant	708	105	+5.71
	Safety instructions	797	111	
9582421	Device, Electric motor	4,920	730	+10.96
	Assembly instructions	5,850	810	
9582422	Production plant	4,840	750	+8.40
	Traffic instructions	6,010	813	
9582423	Device, Filter	8,069	1,230	+10.57
	Set up instructions	10,538	1,360	
9582424	Substance, Manufacturing process	5,837	960	+12.50
	Industrial standards	7,138	1,080	
9582425	Device, Maintenance, check, repair	6,690	1,010	+9.90
	Instructions	8,490	1,110	
9582426	Substance, Manufacturing process	12,410	1,880	+11.70
	Patent	14,420	2,100	
9582427	Production plant	46,908	6,760	+7.10
	Traffic instructions	51,059	7,240	
9582428	Production plant	1,367	217	+12.44
	Safety instructions	1,538	244	
9582429	Substance, Manufacturing process	14,290	2,240	+8.48
	Patent	16,420	2,430	
9582430	Device, Pneumatic installation	12,744	1,890	+5.19
	Safety instructions	14,346	1,988	
Subtotal Percentage (A)				**+469.65**
Subtotal Mean Value of Percentage (A : 30 =)				**+15.66**

Specialty field: Chemistry, process engineering, plant engineering, patents				
RNo.	Specifications	Characters with spaces	Number of words	% Number of words
9582431	Substance, Manufacturing process	6,081	943	+21.95
	Industrial standards	7,576	1,150	
9582432	Substance, Manufacturing process	819	134	+17.91
	Industrial standards	954	158	
9582433	Production plant	820	131	+14.50
	Industrial standards	947	150	
9582434	Substance, Manufacturing process	533	84	+20.24
	Industrial standards	641	101	
9582435	Production plant	737	111	+18.92
	Industrial standards	928	132	
9582436	Substance, Manufacturing process	4,762	859	+29.34
	Industrial standards	6,311	1,111	
9582437	Plant engineering	1,292	229	+19.21
	Safety instructions	1,600	273	
9582438	Substance, Manufacturing process	1,436	275	+23.64
	Industrial standards	1,905	340	
9582439	Plant engineering	4,152	747	+18.34
	Industrial standards	4,940	884	
9582440	Substance, Manufacturing process	6,062	1,125	+14.67
	Safety instructions	8,079	1,290	
9582441	Production plant	20,125	3,735	+5.76
	Safety instructions	26,823	3,950	
9582442	Substance, Manufacturing process	1,926	363	+13.77
	Industrial standards	2,328	413	
9582443	Substance, Manufacturing process	2,008	398	+10.30
	Safety instructions	2,640	439	
9582444	Plant engineering	830	156	+5.77
	Safety instructions	1,068	165	
9582445	Substance, Manufacturing process	5,622	1,015	+11.92
	Safety instructions	7,175	1,136	
9582446	Production plant	690	150	+13.33
	Industrial standards	720	170	
9582447	Plant engineering	45,080	8,366	+5.69
	Safety instructions	60,083	8,842	
9582448	Substance, Manufacturing process	2,239	421	+7.13
	Safety instructions	2,908	451	
9582449	Plant engineering	4,497	891	+4.83
	Safety instructions	5,914	934	
9582450	Substance, Manufacturing process	12,593	2,273	+3.12
	Patent	16,072	2,344	
Subtotal Percentage (B)				+280.34
Subtotal Mean Value of Percentage (B : 20 =)				+14.02
Total Amount Percentage (C)				+749.99
Total Amount Mean Value of Percentage (C : 50 =)				+15.00

The mean value of percentage for translations EN => ES in the area of chemistry is +15.00. According to the defined tolerance it can be rounded to +15.00. Maximum divergence values here are: +45.40 and +3.12.

A text of 100 words in the source language will probably have approx. 115 words in the target language.

RNo.	Specifications	Characters with spaces	Number of words	% Number of words
9583001	Substance, Manufacturing process	6,301	1,046	-25.43
	Production	5,276	780	
9583002	Plant engineering	2,049	369	-33.06
	Safety instructions	1,698	247	
9583003	Plant engineering	3,420	650	-33.85
	Safety instructions	2,750	430	
9583004	Plant engineering	6,245	1,096	-26.19
	Safety instructions	5,383	809	
9583005	Substance, Manufacturing process	29,630	5,230	-38.81
	Patent	26,290	3,200	
9583006	Plant engineering	1,070	177	-36.16
	Safety instructions	946	113	
9583007	Plant engineering	871	158	-39.24
	Safety instructions	634	96	
9583008	Plant engineering	1,426	252	-6.35
	Safety instructions	1,440	236	
9583009	Plant engineering	763	148	-14.86
	Safety instructions	830	126	
9583010	Plant engineering	673	132	-9.09
	Safety instructions	716	120	
9583011	Plant engineering	2,283	416	-29.09
	Safety instructions	2,036	295	
9583012	Plant engineering	7,332	1,324	-33.23
	Safety instructions	6,619	884	
9583013	Plant engineering	5,918	1,058	-43.01
	Safety instructions	5,667	603	
9583014	Device, Maintenance, check, repair	3,088	523	-38.24
	Instructions	2,319	323	
9583015	Device, Maintenance, check, repair	1,905	340	-37.65
	Instructions	1,637	212	
9583016	Device, Maintenance, check, repair	916	164	-31.71
	Instructions	750	112	
9583017	Substance, Manufacturing process	421	67	-37.31
	Production	351	42	
9583018	Substance, Manufacturing process	17,305	3,108	-35.00
	Patent	14,990	2,020	
9583019	Plant engineering	766	128	-35.16
	Traffic instructions	597	83	
9583020	Substance, Manufacturing process	6,520	1,096	-35.22
	Production	5,670	710	
9583021	Plant engineering	1,432	241	-38.17
	Safety instructions	1,133	149	
9583022	Substance, Manufacturing process	3,376	571	-36.08
	Production	2,997	365	
9583023	Plant engineering	2,104	281	-40.21
	Safety instructions	2,024	168	
9583024	Substance, Manufacturing process	987	304	-38.16
	Production	927	188	
9583025	Substance, Manufacturing process	15,354	2,536	-37.03
	Patent	13,581	1,597	
9583026	Plant engineering	1,098	174	-35.06
	Safety instructions	1,055	113	
9583027	Substance, Manufacturing process	1,460	250	-36.00
	Production	1,312	160	
9583028	Plant engineering	12,103	1,978	-40.04
	Safety instructions	9,694	1,186	
9583029	Substance, Manufacturing process	1,549	171	-60.23
	Production	1,274	68	
9583030	Plant engineering	4,586	760	-56.05
	Traffic instructions	4,125	334	
Subtotal Percentage (A)				-1,035.69
Subtotal Mean Value of Percentage (A : 30 =)				-34.52

RNo.	Specifications	Characters with spaces	Number of words	% Number of words
	Expansion/compression factor for translations from Spanish (ES) into German (DE)			
	Specialty field: Chemistry, process engineering, plant engineering, patents			
9583031	Substance, Manufacturing process	5,107	847	-48.05
	Production	2,785	440	
9583032	Plant engineering	384	72	-37.50
	Traffic instructions	310	45	
9583033	Substance, Manufacturing process	6,889	1,148	-38.07
	Production	6,008	711	
9583034	Plant engineering	1,313	228	-36.40
	Traffic instructions	1,110	145	
9583035	Substance, Manufacturing process	1,724	299	-36.12
	Production	1,423	191	
9583036	Plant engineering	1,391	226	-37.17
	Safety instructions	1,251	142	
9583037	Substance, Manufacturing process	1,555	253	-37.15
	Production	1,205	159	
9583038	Substance, Manufacturing process	3,237	522	-31.99
	Production	2,851	355	
9583039	Plant engineering	1,115	177	-35.03
	Safety instructions	955	115	
9583040	Substance, Manufacturing process	1,396	218	-29.82
	Production	1,220	153	
9583041	Plant engineering	1,377	209	-35.41
	Safety instructions	1,119	135	
9583042	Substance, Manufacturing process	1,351	207	-34.78
	Production	1,077	135	
9583043	Plant engineering	1,381	233	-34.76
	Safety instructions	1,223	152	
9583044	Substance, Manufacturing process	1,779	282	-34.75
	Production	1,433	184	
9583045	Substance, Manufacturing process	1,131	180	-35.00
	Production	938	117	
9583046	Plant engineering	744	133	-34.59
	Safety instructions	686	87	
9583047	Substance, Manufacturing process	7,397	1,235	-34.74
	Production	6,432	806	
9583048	Plant engineering	984	164	-34.76
	Traffic instructions	787	107	
9583049	Plant engineering	1,270	214	-34.58
	Safety instructions	1,032	140	
9583050	Substance, Manufacturing process	6,247	1,034	-33.94
	Production	5,543	683	
Subtotal Percentage (B)				-714.61
Subtotal Mean Value of Percentage (B : 20 =)				-35.73
Total Amount Percentage (C)				-1,750.30
Total Amount Mean Value of Percentage (C : 50 =)				-35.00

The mean value of percentage for translations ES => DE in the area of chemistry is -35.00. According to the defined tolerance it can be rounded to -35.00. Maximum divergence values here are: -6.35 and –60.23.

A text of 100 words in the source language will probably have approx. 65 words in the target language.

RNo.	Specifications	Characters with spaces	Number of words	% Number of words
Expansion/compression factor for translations from Spanish (ES) into English (EN)				Page – 1
Specialty field: Chemistry, process engineering, plant engineering, patents				
9583151	Substance, Manufacturing process	3,578	524	-4.39
	Industrial standards	3,379	501	
9583152	Production plant	1,689	247	-15.79
	Industrial standards	1,493	208	
9583153	Production plant	4,288	631	-10.62
	Industrial standards	4,339	564	
9583154	Plant engineering	3,857	564	-15.78
	Safety instructions	3,410	475	
9583155	Plant engineering	3,720	542	-6.83
	Safety instructions	3,682	505	
9583156	Production plant	3,331	487	-13.96
	Industrial standards	3,008	419	
9583157	Plant engineering	1,985	333	-25.22
	Safety instructions	1,503	249	
9583158	Production plant	5,581	816	-15.20
	Industrial standards	4,968	692	
9583159	Plant engineering	4,017	630	-23.97
	Safety instructions	3,680	479	
9583160	Production plant	5,020	734	-16.21
	Industrial standards	4,415	615	
9583161	Plant engineering	1,573	269	-23.42
	Safety instructions	1,377	206	
9583162	Production plant	1,067	156	-14.10
	Industrial standards	962	134	
9583163	Substance, Manufacturing process	63,412	9,800	-19.81
	Patent	55,947	7,859	
9583164	Plant engineering	9,357	1,368	-14.77
	Safety instructions	8,371	1,166	
9583165	Plant engineering	1,278	215	-14.88
	Safety instructions	1,042	183	
9583166	Production plant	2,373	347	-16.43
	Industrial standards	2,082	290	
9583167	Production plant	2,051	350	-15.14
	Industrial standards	1,753	297	
9583168	Production plant	1,155	169	-20.71
	Industrial standards	961	134	
9583169	Production plant	2,028	336	-19.64
	Industrial standards	1,825	270	
9583170	Production plant	2,448	358	-15.64
	Industrial standards	2,168	302	
9583171	Production plant	1,973	314	-11.46
	Industrial standards	1,544	278	
9583172	Substance, Manufacturing process	1,222	192	-10.94
	Industrial standards	1,058	171	
9583173	Plant engineering	4,393	680	-15.88
	Safety instructions	4,152	572	
9583174	Production plant	341	55	-9.09
	Safety instructions	334	50	
9583175	Production plant	11,376	1,924	-14.34
	Safety instructions	9,716	1,648	
9583176	Production plant	2,130	352	-14.49
	Safety instructions	1,797	301	
9583177	Production plant	2,444	413	-14.53
	Safety instructions	2,044	353	
9583178	Production plant	1,296	231	-14.72
	Safety instructions	1,037	197	
9583179	Production plant	1,557	271	-15.50
	Safety instructions	1,315	229	
9583180	Production plant	697	118	-6.78
	Safety instructions	566	110	
Subtotal Percentage (A)				-450.24
Subtotal Mean Value of Percentage (A : 30 =)				-15.01

RNo.	Specifications	Characters with spaces	Number of words	% Number of words
Expansion/compression factor for translations from Spanish (ES) into English (EN)				Page – 2
Specialty field: Chemistry, process engineering, plant engineering, patents				
9583181	Production plant	1,500	237	-8.86
	Industrial standards	1,295	216	
9583182	Device, Maintenance, check, repair	241	35	-17.14
	Instructions	213	29	
9583183	Device, Maintenance, check, repair	1,606	247	-15.38
	Instructions	1,424	209	
9583184	Plant engineering	1,439	231	-15.58
	Traffic instructions	1,155	195	
9583185	Substance, Manufacturing process	20,702	3,431	-23.60
	Patent	18,471	2,621	
9583186	Device, Maintenance, check, repair	1,062	176	-14.20
	Instructions	978	151	
9583187	Plant engineering	4,428	760	-8.03
	Traffic instructions	3,805	699	
9583188	Plant engineering	2,760	460	-14.13
	Traffic instructions	2,432	395	
9583189	Device, Maintenance, check, repair	1,628	258	-14.34
	Instructions	1,498	221	
9583190	Substance, Manufacturing process	1,380	226	-15.04
	Safety instructions	1,268	192	
9583191	Device, Maintenance, check, repair	1,215	215	-14.42
	Instructions	1,075	184	
9583192	Device, Maintenance, check, repair	8,207	1,392	-15.09
	Instructions	7,074	1,182	
9583193	Substance, Manufacturing process	1,040	176	-15.34
	Production	917	149	
9583194	Substance, Manufacturing process	16,620	2,896	-17.67
	Patent	13,894	2,384	
9583195	Production plant	1,160	189	-15.34
	Industrial standards	1,059	160	
9583196	Production plant	1,224	204	-16.67
	Industrial standards	1,082	170	
9583197	Production plant	920	156	-13.46
	Safety instructions	826	135	
9583198	Plant engineering	860	151	-15.89
	Safety instructions	722	127	
9583199	Plant engineering	605	101	-14.85
	Safety instructions	517	86	
9583200	Device, Maintenance, check, repair	1,252	210	-14.76
	Instructions	1,029	178	
Subtotal Percentage (B)				-299.79
Subtotal Mean Value of Percentage (B : 20 =)				-14.99
Total Amount Percentage (C)				-750.03
Total Amount Mean Value of Percentage (C : 50 =)				-15.00

The mean value of percentage for translations ES => EN in the area of chemistry is -15.00. According to the defined tolerance it can be rounded to -15.00. Maximum divergence values here are: -4.39 and –25.22.

A text of 100 words in the source language will probably have approx. -85 words in the target language.

RNo.	Specifications	Characters with spaces	Number of words	% Number of words
	Expansion/compression factor for translations from German (DE) into English (EN)			**Page – 1**
	Specialty field: Precision mechanics, automatic control systems, patents			
9330001	Engine	249,222	30,542	+19.80
	Assembly instructions	230,513	36,589	
9330002	Product, Distribution and marketing	283,628	34,758	+21.00
	Product information	261,897	42,059	
9330003	Engine	25,128	3,079	+17.99
	Operating instructions	26,206	3,633	
9330004	Engine	57,988	7,106	+22.42
	Operating instructions	72,485	8,699	
9330005	Spare part	44,833	5,494	+19.00
	Assembly instructions	43,940	6,538	
9330006	Engine	16,647	2,039	+19.32
	Operating instructions	16,680	2,433	
9330007	Spare part	24,505	3,003	+21.38
	Assembly instructions	26,075	3,645	
9330008	Product, Distribution and marketing	5,061	620	+19.52
	Product information	4,963	741	
9330009	Engine	18,254	2,237	+22.84
	Assembly instructions	22,470	2,748	
9330010	Spare part	9,009	1,104	+17.93
	Assembly instructions	9,033	1,302	
9330011	Product, Distribution and marketing	3,144	385	+21.82
	Product information	3,807	469	
9330012	Engine	4,490	550	+16.73
	Operating instructions	4,725	642	
9330013	Product, Manufacturing process	1,029,586	126,174	+19.99
	Patent	945,139	151,400	
9330014	Product, Distribution and marketing	33,731	4,131	+24.59
	Product information	32,438	5,147	
9330015	Product, Manufacturing process	934,132	114,476	+19.98
	Patent	858,234	137,351	
9330016	Engine	23,688	3,952	+19.48
	Operating instructions	27,480	4,722	
9330017	Engine	29,003	4,568	+18.59
	Operating instructions	33,379	5,417	
9330018	Spare part	74,391	12,487	+23.19
	Assembly instructions	84,557	15,383	
9330019	Product, Manufacturing process	183,928	22,540	+20.51
	Patent	169,552	27,164	
9330020	Product, Distribution and marketing	21,521	3,868	+17.58
	Product information	24,261	4,548	
9330021	Engine	9,490	1,593	+18.71
	Assembly instructions	10,788	1,891	
9330022	Engine	597,844	73,265	+22.70
	Safety instructions	549,269	89,896	
9330023	Engine	16,081	1,971	+20.40
	Operating instructions	16,771	2,373	
9330024	Product, Distribution and marketing	13,348	1,683	+15.63
	Product information	13,920	1,946	
9330025	Product, Manufacturing process	262,519	32,171	+20.31
	Patent	247,880	38,705	
9330026	Spare part	42,056	5,727	+21.30
	Assembly instructions	36,644	6,947	
9330027	Engine	24,534	3,431	+19.99
	Assembly instructions	26,790	4,117	
9330028	Product, Manufacturing process	478,782	58,674	+18.00
	Patent	448,384	69,235	
9330029	Spare part	35,602	5,240	+25.31
	Assembly instructions	38,361	6,566	
9330030	Product, Distribution and marketing	9,870	1,410	+15.25
	Product information	10,584	1,625	
Subtotal Percentage (A)				**+601.26**
Subtotal Mean Value of Percentage (A : 30 =)				**+20.04**

RNo.	Specifications	Characters with spaces	Number of words	% Number of words
	Expansion/compression factor for translations from German (DE) into English (EN)			**Page – 2**
	Specialty field: Precision mechanics, automatic control systems, patents			
9330031	Engine	10,358	1,419	+20.86
	Operating instructions	10,650	1,715	
9330032	Spare part	49,820	9,047	+20.29
	Assembly instructions	56,150	10,883	
9330033	Product, Manufacturing process	20,510	2,513	+20.97
	Patent	19,163	3,040	
9330034	Manufacturing process	37,160	4,564	+18.60
	Industrial standards	38,754	5,413	
9330035	Product, Distribution and marketing	55,193	6,793	+19.30
	Product information	52,724	8,104	
9330036	Spare part	74,137	13,587	+19.30
	Assembly instructions	83,307	16,209	
9330037	Product, Manufacturing process	27,613	3,384	+20.27
	Patent	25,583	4,070	
9330038	Product, Distribution and marketing	10,384	1,282	+19.81
	Product information	10,926	1,536	
9330039	Spare part	7,958	1,479	+19.20
	Assembly instructions	9,004	1,763	
9330040	Engine	15,435	1,919	+20.95
	Assembly instructions	16,240	2,321	
9330041	Manufacturing process	15,435	1920	+20.10
	Industrial standards	16,240	2,306	
9330042	Engine	16,588	2,082	+19.69
	Safety instructions	17,488	2,492	
9330043	Product, Manufacturing process	33,731	4,131	+20.99
	Patent	32,434	4,998	
9330044	Spare part	10,523	1,978	+20.02
	Assembly instructions	13,667	2,374	
9330045	Product, Distribution and marketing	26,423	4,770	+19.20
	Product information	33,722	5,686	
9330046	Manufacturing process	9,437	1,823	+19.25
	Industrial standards	12,408	2,174	
9330047	Engine	3,901	733	+19.37
	Safety instructions	5,019	875	
9330048	Product, Distribution and marketing	28,491	5,287	+19.39
	Product information	37,971	6,312	
9330049	Product, Manufacturing process	327,588	40,643	+21.00
	Patent	306,244	49,178	
9330050	Spare part	20,355	3,510	+20.28
	Assembly instructions	23,500	4,222	
Subtotal Percentage (B)				**+398.84**
Subtotal Mean Value of Percentage (B : 20 =)				**+19.94**
Total Amount Percentage (C)				**+1,000.10**
Total Amount Mean Value of Percentage (C : 50 =)				**+20.00**

The mean value of percentage for translations DE => EN in the area of precision mechanics is +20.00. According to the defined tolerance it can be rounded to +20.00. Maximum divergence values here are: +25.31 and +15.25.

A text of 100 words in the source language will probably have approx. 120 words in the target language.

RNo.	Specifications	Characters with spaces	Number of words	% Number of words
9330151	Device, Servo motor	12.752	1.827	+40.72
	Operating instructions	14.481	2.571	
9330152	Spare part	1.111	163	+38.65
	Assembly instructions	1.269	226	
9330153	Engine	39.300	5.300	+45.28
	Assembly instructions	44.200	7.700	
9330154	Spare part	5.276	780	+34.10
	Assembly instructions	6.301	1.046	
9330155	Device, Feed-off-the-arm	1.698	247	+40.08
	Assembly instructions	2.049	346	
9330156	Device, Compact AC servo motor	2.750	430	+39.07
	Assembly instructions	3.420	598	
9330157	Spare part	5.383	809	+35.47
	Assembly instructions	6.285	1.096	
9330158	Device, Filter regulator	2.629	422	+23.93
	Assembly instructions	2.963	523	
9330159	Spare part	946	133	+33.08
	Assembly instructions	1.070	177	
9330160	Device, Small-sized cylinder bed	634	96	+55.21
	Assembly instructions	871	149	
9330161	Spare part	1.440	236	+6.77
	Assembly instructions	1.426	252	
9330162	Device, Thread trimmer	830	136	+8.82
	Assembly instructions	763	148	
9330163	Spare part	716	124	+6.45
	Assembly instructions	673	132	
9330164	Device, Solenoid valve	2.036	295	+41.01
	Assembly instructions	2.283	416	
9330165	Spare part	6.619	984	+34.55
	Assembly instructions	7.332	1.324	
9330166	Device, Air lines for pneumatic knife	5.667	893	+18.47
	Assembly instructions	5.918	1.058	
9330167	Device, Pneumatic presser foot lift	2.319	323	+51.08
	Assembly instructions	3.088	488	
9330168	Spare part	597	82	+56.09
	Assembly instructions	766	128	
9330169	Product, Manufacturing process	14.980	2.363	+31.57
	Patent	17.305	3.109	
9330170	Device, Driving system	1.029	151	+39.07
	Assembly instructions	1.252	210	
9330171	Spare part	722	102	+48.03
	Assembly instructions	860	151	
9330172	Device, Upper knife stopper adjustment	517	79	+27.84
	Assembly instructions	600	101	
9330173	Engine	826	109	+43.11
	Operating instructions	920	156	
9330174	Device, Under thread holder adjustment	1.059	151	+25.16
	Assembly instructions	1.160	189	
9330175	Engine	1.082	140	+45.71
	Operating instructions	1.224	204	
9330176	Engine	897	122	+53.27
	Operating instructions	1.073	187	
9330177	Engine	7.074	953	+40.92
	Operating instructions	8.207	1.343	
9330178	Engine	917	119	+47.89
	Operating instructions	1.040	176	
9330179	Device, Electric needle thread wiper	1.075	164	+31.09
	Assembly instructions	1.215	215	
9330180	Engine	1.498	201	+28.35
	Operating instructions	1.628	258	
Subtotal Percentage (A)				**+1,070.84**
Subtotal Mean Value of Percentage (A : 30 =)				**+35.69**

Expansion/compression factor for translations from German (DE) into Spanish (ES) — Page – 1

Specialty field: Precision mechanics, automatic control systems, patents

RNo.	Specifications	Characters with spaces	Number of words	% Number of words
	Expansion/compression factor for translations from German (DE) into Spanish (ES)			Page – 2
	Specialty field: Precision mechanics, automatic control systems, patents			
9330181	Product, Distribution and marketing	1.268	172	+31.39
	Product information	1.380	226	
9330182	Engine	2.432	355	+29.57
	Operating instructions	2.760	460	
9330183	Engine	3.805	499	+52.30
	Operating instructions	4.428	760	
9330184	Product, Distribution and marketing	978	141	+24.82
	Product information	1.062	176	
9330185	Device, Filter	18.471	2.421	+41.71
	Assembly instructions	20.702	3.431	
9330186	Product, Distribution and marketing	1.155	159	+45.28
	Product information	1.439	231	
9330187	Product, Distribution and marketing	213	29	+20.68
	Product information	241	35	
9330188	Engine	1.424	189	+30.68
	Safety instructions	1.606	247	
9330189	Product, Distribution and marketing	566	77	+53.24
	Product information	697	118	
9330190	Product, Distribution and marketing	1.295	176	+34.65
	Product information	1.500	237	
9330191	Product, Distribution and marketing	1.797	261	+34.86
	Product information	2.130	352	
9330192	Product, Distribution and marketing	2.044	303	+36.30
	Product information	2.444	413	
9330193	Device, Filter	9.257	1.603	+6.48
	Assembly instructions	8.702	1.707	
9330194	Engine	9.716	1.348	+42.72
	Operating instructions	11.376	1.924	
9330195	Engine	3.253	487	+9.85
	Safety instructions	3.321	535	
9330196	Spare part	4.152	532	+27.81
	Assembly instructions	4.393	680	
9330197	Engine	1.058	151	+27.15
	Operating instructions	1.222	192	
9330198	Product, Distribution and marketing	1.037	147	+57.14
	Product information	1.296	231	
9330199	Product, Distribution and marketing	1.315	189	+43.38
	Product information	1.557	271	
9330200	Device, Belt cover	1.825	260	+29.23
	Assembly instructions	2.028	336	
Subtotal Percentage (B)				+679.24
Subtotal Mean Value of Percentage (B : 20 =)				+33.96
Total Amount Percentage (C)				+1,750.08
Total Amount Mean Value of Percentage (C : 50 =)				+35.00

The mean value of percentage for translations DE => ES in the area of precision mechanics is +35.00. According to the defined tolerance it can be rounded to +35.00. Maximum divergence values here are: +6.45 and +57.14.

A text of 100 words in the source language will probably have approx. 135 words in the target language.

RNo.	Specifications	Characters with spaces	Number of words	% Number of words
	Expansion/compression factor for translations from English (EN) into German (DE)			Page – 1
	Specialty field: Precision mechanics, automatic control systems, patents			
9330251	Modular slots	3.466	597	-15.07
	Assembly instructions	3.652	507	
9330252	Engine	6.350	1.055	-14.69
	Assembly instructions	6.909	900	
9330253	Engine	37,167	6,333	-20.64
	Service manual	37,180	5,026	
9330254	Tools, Manufacturing process	3,780	644	-28.73
	Instructions	3,365	459	
9330255	Engine, Manufacturing process	49,060	8,359	-22.60
	Safety instructions	49,077	6,470	
9330256	Engine	8,971	1,528	-13.87
	Operating instructions	9,654	1,316	
9330257	Engine	37,167	6,333	-20.83
	Service manual	37,180	5,014	
9330258	Engine, Manufacturing process	22,316	3,802	-29.93
	Safety instructions	19,560	2,664	
9330259	Engine	27,033	4,606	-14.35
	Operating instructions	29,108	3,945	
9330260	Engine, Manufacturing process	4,928	840	-12.02
	Safety instructions	5,420	739	
9330261	Engine, Manufacturing process	28,157	4,798	-20.07
	Safety instructions	28,166	3,835	
9330262	Engine	25,900	4,412	-18.90
	Operating instructions	26,264	3,578	
9330263	Engine, Manufacturing process	12,605	1,932	-20.03
	Safety instructions	11,216	1,545	
9330264	Engine, Manufacturing process	12,146	2,049	-30.89
	Safety instructions	10,673	1,416	
9330265	Engine, Manufacturing process	12,376	2,016	-24.75
	Safety instructions	10,768	1,517	
9330266	Engine	34,567	5,889	-28.95
	Operating instructions	30,299	4,184	
9330267	Engine	26,725	4,553	-22.82
	Operating instructions	26,734	3,514	
9330268	Tools, Manufacturing process	62,300	10,516	-20.12
	Instructions	57,920	8,400	
9330269	Tools, Manufacturing process	42,268	7,201	-21.44
	Instructions	42,862	5,657	
9330270	Tools, Manufacturing process	34,193	5,826	-21.73
	Instructions	34,205	4,560	
9330271	Memory options	61,689	10,505	-28.59
	Assembly instructions	54,924	7,502	
9330272	Engine	46,939	7,996	-24.92
	Operating instructions	48,132	6,003	
9330273	Modules	48,630	8,170	-3.35
	Assembly instructions	58,049	7,896	
9330274	Engine, Manufacturing process	16,564	2,822	-14.24
	Safety instructions	17,836	2,420	
9330275	Memory options	54,180	8,898	-14.34
	Assembly instructions	59,404	7,622	
9330276	Memory options	43,652	7,436	-19,63
	Assembly instructions	48,048	5,976	
9330277	Memory options	35,560	5,908	-18.26
	Assembly instructions	38,690	4,829	
9330278	Memory options	17,253	2,940	-20.00
	Assembly instructions	17,259	2,352	
9330279	Memory options	19,409	3,343	-18.49
	Assembly instructions	20,451	2,725	
9330280	Memory options	8,545	1,456	-16.14
	Assembly instructions	6,412	1,221	
Subtotal Percentage (A)				-600.39
Subtotal Mean Value of Percentage (A : 30 =)				-20.01

RNo.	Specifications	Characters with spaces	Number of words	% Number of words
	Expansion/compression factor for translations from English (EN) into German (DE)			Page – 2
	Specialty field: Precision mechanics, automatic control systems, patents			
9330281	Security information management	34,557	5,885	-5.86
	Assembly instructions	40,706	5,540	
9330282	Upgrade licenses	56,397	9,696	-12.43
	Legal instructions	66,432	8,490	
9330283	Packing platform support	8,522	1,454	-12.04
	Product information	7,347	1,279	
9330284	Technology identifiers	10,970	1,696	-16.45
	Assembly instructions	10,304	1,417	
9330285	Analysis modules	2,206	352	-22.16
	Assembly instructions	2,167	274	
9330286	Secure user registration tool	78,971	13,468	-20.00
	Assembly instructions	71,517	10,774	
9330287	Transport manager	58,839	9,514	-24.07
	Assembly instructions	52,595	7,224	
9330288	Multiservice swiching platform	8,954	1,478	-20.43
	Assembly instructions	7,800	1,176	
9330289	Multiservice transport platform	5,902	1,041	-22.00
	Assembly instructions	5,409	812	
9330290	Extended services platform	7,593	1,192	-21.14
	Assembly instructions	6,636	940	
9330291	Fiber amplifier	11,524	1,842	-22.20
	Assembly instructions	9,643	1,433	
9330292	Multiservice provisioning platforms	9,318	1,450	-20.76
	Assembly instructions	7,929	1,149	
9330293	Multiservice access platforms	7,117	1,215	-24.44
	Assembly instructions	6,720	918	
9330294	Aggregation platform	8,971	1,400	-19.43
	Assembly instructions	7,504	1,128	
9330295	Optical transmission	19,723	3,337	-25.68
	Assembly instructions	17,186	2,480	
9330296	Tools, Manufacturing process	13,895	2,168	-21.45
	Instructions	11,623	1,703	
9330297	Hosting solution engine	11,653	1,881	-22.01
	Assembly instructions	10,354	1,467	
9330298	Policy manager	7,604	1,293	-27.30
	Assembly instructions	6,473	940	
9330299	Telephony environment manager	7,733	1,394	-19.66
	Assembly instructions	6,428	1,120	
9330300	Voice manager	7,851	1,192	-20.13
	Assembly instructions	6,944	952	
Subtotal Percentage (B)				-399.64
Subtotal Mean Value of Percentage (B : 20 =)				-19.98
Total Amount Percentage (C)				-1,000.03
Total Amount Mean Value of Percentage (C : 50 =)				-20.00

The mean value of percentage for translations EN => DE in the area of precision mechanics is -20.00. According to the defined tolerance it can be rounded to -20.00. Maximum divergence values here are: -3.35 and –30.89.

A text of 100 words in the source language will probably have approx. 80 words in the target language.

RNo.	Specifications	Characters with spaces	Number of words	% Number of words
	Expansion/compression factor for translations from English (EN) into Spanish (ES)			Page – 1
	Specialty field: Precision mechanics, automatic control systems, patents			
9330401	Device, Power optic cable	11.240	1.720	+16.86
	Assembly instructions	13.880	2.010	
9330402	Engine	12.320	1.890	+23.80
	Service Manual	15.030	2.340	
9330403	Engine	4.740	660	+15.15
	Assembly instructions	5.200	760	
9330404	Engine	18.400	2.530	+19.76
	Assembly instructions	19.590	3.030	
9330405	Engine	6.720	1.070	+26.16
	Service instructions	8.880	1.350	
9330406	Tools, Manufacturing process	7.750	1.190	+11.76
	Instructions	8.920	1.330	
9330407	Engine, Manufacturing process	6.430	1.010	+29.70
	Safety instructions	8.240	1.300	
9330408	Engine	9.090	1.420	+22.53
	Service Manual	11.610	1.740	
9330409	Engine, Manufacturing process	4.470	640	+12.19
	Safety instructions	4.830	718	
9330410	Tools, Manufacturing process	5.860	920	+15.21
	Instructions	6.940	1.060	
9330411	Extended services platform	6.720	1.010	+16.83
	Assembly instructions	7.960	1.180	
9330412	Engine	3.870	510	+23.53
	Assembly instructions	3.940	630	
9330413	Engine	6.390	930	+11.61
	Service manual	7.346	1.038	
9330414	Tools, Manufacturing process I	10.970	1.660	+5.90
	Instructions	11.950	1.758	
9330415	Tools, Manufacturing process	12.930	2.020	+8.02
	Instructions	13.706	2.182	
9330416	Engine	8.630	1.400	+27.14
	Assembly instructions	11.070	1.780	
9330417	Tools, Manufacturing process	9.580	1.370	+5.84
	Instructions	10.059	1.450	
9330418	Engine	7.080	1.050	+5.71
	Service manual	7.970	1.110	
9330419	Tools, Manufacturing process	4.920	730	+24.65
	Instructions	5.850	910	
9330420	Tools, Manufacturing process	4.840	750	+33.33
	Instructions	6.010	1.000	
9330421	Engine	8.060	1.230	+6.02
	Operating instructions	8.463	1.304	
9330422	Engine	5.830	960	+22.91
	Operating instructions	7.130	1.180	
9330423	Engine	6.690	1.010	+19.80
	Operating instructions	8.490	1.210	
9330424	Plant	12.410	1.880	+4.15
	Assembly instructions	13.420	1.958	
9330425	Plant	42.690	6.760	+17.45
	Assembly instructions	51.050	7.940	
9330426	Tools, Manufacturing process	13.670	2.170	+12.44
	Instructions	15,380	2.440	
9330427	Engine	14.290	2.240	+17.41
	Service manual	16.420	2.630	
9330428	Power cord 250VAC 2.5Acoupler	6.081	943	+21.95
	Assembly instructions	7.576	1.150	
9330429	Power cord 125VAC 3Acoupler	819	134	+17.91
	Assembly instructions	954	158	
9330430	Power cord plug UK	533	84	+10.71
	Assembly instructions	641	93	
Subtotal Percentage (A)				**+506.43**
Subtotal Mean Value of Percentage (A : 30 =)				**+16.88**

RNo.	Specifications	Characters with spaces	NUmber of words	% Number of words
	Expansion/compression factor for translations from English (EN) into Spanish (ES)			
	Specialty field: Precision mechanics, automatic control systems, patents			
9330431	Power cord plug US	737	111	+18.91
	Assembly instructions	928	132	
9330432	Power cord plug EU	4.762	859	+29.33
	Assembly instructions	6.311	1.111	
9330433	Fibre channel ports	1.292	229	+19.21
	Assembly instructions	1.600	273	
9330434	Fibre channel ports	6.081	943	+12.09
	Assembly instructions	7.076	1.057	
9330435	Fibre channel ports	819	134	+12.69
	Assembly instructions g	954	151	
9330436	Fibre channel ports	533	84	+13.09
	Assembly instructions	641	95	
9330437	Fibre channel ports	737	111	+12.61
	Assembly instructions	928	125	
9330438	Fibre channel ports	4.762	859	+9.08
	Assembly instructions	5.238	937	
9330439	Fibre channel ports	1.292	229	+10.04
	Assembly instructions	1.600	252	
9330440	Fibre channel ports	1.436	275	+11.27
	Assembly instructions	1.637	306	
9330441	Memory options	4.152	747	+9.10
	Assembly instructions	4.940	815	
9330442	Memory options	6.062	1.125	+9.07
	Assembly instructions	6.851	1.227	
9330443	Memory options	1.926	363	+13.77
	Assembly instructions	2.328	413	
9330444	Memory options	2.008	398	+11.05
	Assembly instructions	2.640	442	
9330445	Memory options	830	156	+12.18
	Assembly instructions	1.068	175	
9330446	Memory options	5.622	1.015	+8.08
	Assembly instructions	6.410	1.097	
9330447	Memory options	6.148	962	+11.64
	Assembly instructions	7.009	1.074	
9330448	Memory options	4.860	798	+11.03
	Assembly instructions	5.298	886	
9330449	Memory options	6.180	1.078	+5.01
	Assembly instructions	6.970	1.132	
9330450	Modules	4.380	632	+6.01
	Assembly instructions	4.725	670	
	Subtotal Percentage (B)			+245.26
	Subtotal Mean Value of Percentage (B : 20 =)			+12.26
	Total Amount Percentage (C)			+751.69
	Total Amount Mean Value of Percentage (C : 50 =)			+15.03

The mean value of percentage for translations EN => ES in the area of precision mechanics is +15.03. According to the defined tolerance it can be rounded to +15.00. Maximum divergence values here are: +4.15 and +33.33.

A text of 100 words in the source language will probably have approx. 115 words in the target language.

Expansion/compression factor for translations from Spanish (ES) into German (DE)				Page – 1
Specialty field: Precision mechanics, automatic control systems, patents				
RNo.	Specifications	Characters with spaces	Number of words	% Number of words
9331001	Product, manufacturing process	41,076	6,904	-35.21
	Patent	35,721	4,473	
9331002	Memory options	4,825	806	-35.11
	Assembly instructions	3,761	523	
9331003	Analysis modules	10,902	1,958	-35.03
	Assembly instructions	9,443	1,272	
9331004	Memory options	2,652	422	-37.44
	Assembly instructions	2,211	264	
9331005	Memory options	5,770	1,033	-31.75
	Assembly instructions	4,725	705	
9331006	Analysis modules	12,001	2,142	-37.67
	Assembly instructions	10,313	1,335	
9331007	Memory options	19,454	3,294	-38.25
	Assembly instructions	14,609	2,034	
9331008	Analysis modules	37,283	6,665	-42.99
	Assembly instructions	35,702	3,800	
9331009	Memory options	49,191	8,341	-32.03
	Assembly instructions	41,699	5,669	
9331010	Product, manufacturing process	14,382	2,620	-30.61
	Patent	12,826	1,818	
9331011	Memory options	28,891	4,788	-56.58
	Assembly instructions	25,987	2,079	
9331012	Memory options	9,758	1,077	-60.26
	Assembly instructions	8,026	428	
9331013	Product, manufacturing process	76,248	12,461	-40.05
	Patent	61,072	7,470	
9331014	Memory options	9,198	1,575	-36.51
	Assembly instructions	8,265	1,000	
9331015	Analysis modules	6,917	1,096	-35.22
	Assembly instructions	6,646	710	
9331016	Product, manufacturing process	96,730	15,976	-37.34
	Patent	85,560	10,010	
9331017	Memory options	6,218	1,915	-38.22
	Assembly instructions	5,840	1,183	
9331018	Tools, Manufacturing process	13,255	1,770	-40.34
	Instructions	12,751	1,056	
9331019	Product, manufacturing process	21,268	3,597	-36.34
	Patent	18,881	2,290	
9331020	Memory options	9,021	1,518	-38.21
	Assembly instructions	7,137	938	
9331021	Analysis modules	4,239	831	-9.02
	Assembly instructions	4,510	756	
9331022	Tools, Manufacturing process	4,806	932	-15.02
	Instructions	5,229	792	
9331023	Engine	8,983	1,587	-14.49
	Service Manual	9,072	1,357	
9331024	Engine	5,487	995	-39.29
	Service Manual	3,994	604	
9331025	Analysis modules	6,741	1,115	-36.23
	Assembly instructions	5,959	711	
9331026	Product, manufacturing process	18,666	3,294	-38.19
	Patent	16,562	2,036	
9331027	Product, manufacturing process	39,343	6,904	-27.49
	Patent	33,912	5,006	
9331028	Product, manufacturing process	21,546	4,095	-34.33
	Patent	17,325	2,689	
9331029	Memory options	12,908	2,324	-33.48
	Assembly instructions	10,697	1,546	
9331030	Product, manufacturing process	39,696	6,589	-26.94
	Patent	33,238	4,814	
Subtotal Percentage (A)				-1,049,64
Subtotal Mean Value of Percentage (A : 30 =)				-34.99

RNo.	Specifications	Characters with spaces	Number of words	% Number of words
9331031	Analysis modules	8,675	1,316	-35.79
	Assembly instructions	7,049	845	
9331032	Memory options	8,511	1,304	-35.58
	Assembly instructions	6,785	840	
9331033	Analysis modules	8,700	1,467	-35.04
	Assembly instructions	7,704	953	
9331034	Tools, Manufacturing process	11,207	1,776	-34.80
	Instructions	9,027	1,158	
9331035	Engine	7,125	1,134	-35.01
	Service Manual	5,909	737	
9331036	Multiservice switch	4,687	837	-34.65
	Assembly instructions	4,321	547	
9331037	Product, manufacturing process	46,601	7,780	-34.87
	Patent	40,521	5,067	
9331038	Memory options	6,199	1,033	-34.75
	Assembly instructions	4,958	674	
9331039	Analysis modules	8,001	1,348	-34.57
	Assembly instructions	6,501	882	
9331040	Product, manufacturing process	39,356	6,514	-33.99
	Patent	34,920	4,300	
9331041	Memory options	8,794	1,373	-29.86
	Assembly instructions	7,686	963	
9331042	Analysis modules	7,024	1,115	-35.07
	Assembly instructions	6,016	724	
9331043	Product, manufacturing process	20,393	3,288	-32.06
	Patent	17,961	2,234	
9331044	Memory options	9,796	1,593	-37.22
	Assembly instructions	7,591	1,000	
9331045	Analysis modules	8,763	1,423	-37.46
	Assembly instructions	7,881	890	
9331046	Tools, Manufacturing process	10,861	1,883	-36.27
	Instructions	8,964	1,200	
9331047	Engine	8,271	1,436	-36.56
	Service Manual	6,993	911	
9331048	Product, manufacturing process	43,400	7,232	-38.19
	Patent	37,850	4,470	
9331049	Memory options	2,419	453	-31.13
	Assembly instructions	1,953	312	
9331050	Product, manufacturing process	32,174	5,336	-37.68
	Patent	17,545	3,325	
Subtotal Percentage (B)				**-700.55**
Subtotal Mean Value of Percentage (B : 20 =)				**-35.03**
Total Amount Percentage (C)				**-1,750,19**
Total Amount Mean Value of Percentage (C : 50 =)				**-35.00**

The mean value of percentage for translations ES => DE in the area of precision mechanics is -35.00. According to the defined tolerance it can be rounded to -35.00. Maximum divergence values here are: -9.02 and –60.26.

A text of 100 words in the source language will probably have approx. 65 words in the target language.

	Expansion/compression factor for translations from Spanish (ES) into English (EN)			Page – 1
	Specialty field: Precision mechanics, automatic control systems, patents			
RNo.	Specifications	Characters with spaces	Number of words	% Number of words
9331151	Tools, Manufacturing process	20,318	2,971	-15.65
	Instructions	17,994	2,506	
9331152	Product, manufacturing process	16,832	2,788	-19.62
	Patent	15,147	2,241	
9331153	Memory options	9,586	1,402	-20.68
	Assembly instructions	7,976	1,112	
9331154	Product, manufacturing process	17,023	2,905	-15.15
	Patent	14,549	2,465	
9331155	Product, manufacturing process	19,695	2,880	-16.42
	Patent	17,280	2,407	
9331156	Memory options	10,607	1,784	-14.91
	Assembly instructions	8,648	1,518	
9331157	Product, manufacturing process	77,663	11,354	-15.65
	Patent	69,479	9,577	
9331158	Product, manufacturing process	52,631	8,134	-19.08
	Patent	46.436	6,582	
9331159	Memory options	8,856	1,294	-14.06
	Assembly instructions	7,984	1,112	
9331160	Tools, Manufacturing process	13,055	2,232	-23.43
	Instructions	11,429	1,709	
9331161	Analysis modules	5,785	979	-7.76
	Assembly instructions	4,697	903	
9331162	Tools, Manufacturing process	12,923	2,249	-15.96
	Instructions	10,914	1,890	
9331163	Engine	10,756	1,917	-15.23
	Service Manual	8,607	1,625	
9331164	Product, manufacturing process	20,285	3,427	-15.38
	Patent	16,965	2,900	
9331165	Memory options	17,679	2,921	-14.75
	Assembly instructions	14,915	2,490	
9331166	Product, manufacturing process	94,420	15,969	-14.76
	Patent	80,642	13,612	
9331167	Memory options	2,830	456	-12.72
	Assembly instructions	2,772	398	
9331168	Product, manufacturing process	36,461	5,644	-16.18
	Patent	34,461	4,731	
9331169	Memory options	10,142	1,593	-11.42
	Assembly instructions	8,781	1,411	
9331170	Tools, Manufacturing process	16,375	2,606	-14.01
	Instructions	12,815	2,241	
9331171	Product, manufacturing process	41,666	6,092	-16.25
	Patent	36,644	5,102	
9331172	Product, manufacturing process	33,341	5,229	-14.13
	Patent	30,544	4,490	
9331173	Product, manufacturing process	46,322	6,772	-15.19
	Patent	41,234	5,743	
9331174	Memory options	16,475	2,763	-24.50
	Assembly instructions	12,474	2,086	
9331175	Product, manufacturing process	27,647	4,042	-13.16
	Patent	24,966	3,510	
9331176	Product, manufacturing process	30,876	4,498	-6.65
	Patent	30,560	4,199	
9331177	Product, manufacturing process	32,013	4,681	-15.96
	Patent	28,303	3,934	
9331178	Product, manufacturing process	35,590	5,237	-10.94
	Patent	36,013	4,664	
9331179	Memory options	14,018	2,050	-16.19
	Assembly instructions	12,391	1,718	
9331180	Tools, Manufacturing process	29,697	4,349	-4.57
	Instructions	28,045	4,150	
Subtotal Percentage (A)				-450.41
Subtotal Mean Value of Percentage (A : 30 =)				-15.01

Expansion/compression factor for translations from Spaniscen (ES) into English (EN)				Page – 2
Specialty field: Precision mechanics, automatic control systems, patents				
RNo.	Specifications	Characters with spaces	Number of words	% Number of words
9331181	Tools, Manufacturing process	11,454	1,875	-9.92
	Instructions	10,524	1,689	
9331182	Memory options	13,512	2,141	-14.71
	Assembly instructions	12,433	1,826	
9331183	Product, manufacturing process	22,908	3,818	-14.80
	Patent	20,185	3,253	
9331184	Product, manufacturing process	36,752	6,308	-8.56
	Patent	31,581	5,768	
9331185	Memory options	8,814	1,460	-14.72
	Assembly instructions	8,117	1,245	
9331186	Product, manufacturing process	171,826	28,477	-20.64
	Patent	153,309	22,599	
9331187	Memory options	11,943	1,917	-16.48
	Assembly instructions	9,586	1,601	
9331188	Analysis modules	13,329	2,050	-16.19
	Assembly instructions	11,819	1,718	
9331189	Tools, Manufacturing process	2,000	290	-13.79
	Instructions	1,767	250	
9331190	Tools, Manufacturing process	12,450	1,967	-11.29
	Instructions	10,748	1,745	
9331191	Memory options	10,084	1,784	-14.91
	Assembly instructions	8,922	1,518	
9331192	Analysis modules	10,391	1,743	-15.26
	Assembly instructions	8,540	1,477	
9331193	Product, manufacturing process	68,118	11,553	-15.12
	Patent	58,714	9,806	
9331194	Memory options	5,021	838	-15.75
	Assembly instructions	4,291	706	
9331195	Tools, Manufacturing process	8,632	1,460	-15.89
	Instructions	7,611	1,228	
9331196	Product, manufacturing process	137,946	24,036	-17.81
	Patent	115,320	19,754	
9331197	Memory options	9,628	1,568	-15.88
	Assembly instructions	8,789	1,319	
9331198	Analysis modules	10,159	1,693	-17.19
	Assembly instructions	8,980	1,402	
9331199	Tools, Manufacturing process	7,636	1,294	-14.06
	Instructions	6,855	1,112	
9331200	Tools, Manufacturing process	7,138	1,253	-16.60
	Instructions	5,992	1,045	
Subtotal Percentage (B)				-299.57
Subtotal Mean Value of Percentage (B : 20 =)				-14.98
Total Amount Percentage (C)				-749.98
Total Amount Mean Value of Percentage (C : 50 =)				-15.00

The mean value of percentage for translations ES => EN in the area of precision mechanics is -15.00. According to the defined tolerance it can be rounded to -15.00. Maximum divergence values here are: -4.57 and –24.50.

A text of 100 words in the source language will probably have approx. 85 words in the target language.

Final evaluation of all language combinations in all specialty fields of the study					
Languages	% Animal	% Chemistry	% Mechanics	% Total	Mean value of %
DE => EN	+1,000.52	+999.63	+1,000.10	+3,000.25	+3,000.25 : 150 = +20.0016 ~ **+20.00**
DE => ES	+1,749.96	+1,750.20	+1,750.08	+5,250.24	+5,250.24 : 150 = +35.0016 ~ **+35.00**
EN => DE	-998.54	-999.65	-1,000.03	-2,998.22	-2,998.22 : 150 = -19.9881 ~ **-20.00**
EN => ES	+750.12	+749.99	+751.69	+2,251.80	+2,251.80 : 150 = +15.0120 ~ **+15.00**
ES => DE	-1,750.12	-1,750.30	-1,750.19	-5,250.61	-5,250.61 : 150 = -35.0040 ~ **-35.00**
ES => EN	-751.33	-750.03	-749.98	-2,251.34	-2,251.34 : 150 = -15.0089 ~ **-15.00**

The present study only identified the corresponding expansion or compression factor for translations from and into the selected languages as previously intended. It cannot be used for evaluating the quality of a translation, which depends decisively on the qualification and the skill of the translator.